Knitted Toys

Knitted Toys

21 easy-to-knit patterns for irresistible soft toys

FIONA MCTAGUE

BARRON'S

For Lucy and Molly

First edition for the United States and Canada published in 2004 by
Barron's Educational Series, Inc.

First published in 2004 by
New Holland Publishers (UK) Ltd
London • Cape Town • Sydney • Auckland

All inquiries should be addressed to:
Barron's Educational Series, Inc.
250 Wireless Boulevard
Hauppauge, NY 11788
http://www.barronseduc.com

International Standard Book Number: 0-7641-5766-3
Library of Congress Catalog Card Number: 2003112715

Senior Editor: **Clare Sayer**
Production: **Hazel Kirkman**
Designer: **Lisa Tai**
Photographer: **Shona Wood**
Illustrations: **Carrie Hill**
Charts: **Kuo Kang Chen**
Editorial Direction: **Rosemary Wilkinson**

9 8 7 6 5 4 3 2 1

Reproduction by Pica Digital PTE Ltd, Singapore
Printed and bound by Times Offset (M) Sdn Bhd,
Malaysia

Contents

Introduction

My first memory of knitting was as a child on vacation in Scotland, visiting my grandmother. Using scraps of yarn, I knitted little teddy bears and made outfits for them and since then I have been hooked.

I have always been interested in art, textiles, fashion and knitwear which led me to study Fashion and Textiles. I chose to do a collection specializing in knitwear and have not looked back since.

This book is a delightful collection of over 20 adorable designs for soft toys. Knitted in beautiful soft yarns, they will be cherished by babies, young children, and adults alike. Knitted toys make wonderful gifts and will be appreciated so much more than some of the expensive and mass-produced toys in the stores. Some of the designs are delightfully simple, while others will appeal to more experienced knitters and a helpful "skill level" indicator will help you decide where to start. Each project has been beautifully photographed and includes all the information you need on measurements, materials and gauge, as well as full knitting instructions.

Close-up details of the toys help illustrate the patterns even further. There are some projects simple enough to encourage a child to knit, such as the striped scarf or knitted sweater for a favorite teddy bear – perhaps they could go on to knit the teddy itself.

Throughout this book a wonderful palette of quality yarns have been selected, including tweeds, kidsilk, merino pure wools, and cottons.

I've used a whole spectrum of colors, from bold, vibrant primary colors of bright orange, blue, and green, to a more soft chalky pastel range of lilac, soft pink, and muted blue.

The bright yellow cuddly duck, or cute baby pink piglet will become a toddler's best friend. Dressing up the pale pink loveable rag dolls and colorful clown will give the older child hours of fun. A perfect gift for a favorite friend would be the pretty fairy, knitted in a soft white silk haze dress, and trimmed with a silver yarn to give an extra special finishing touch.

Full knitting and finishing instructions are provided in the techniques section of the book, along with diagrams and illustrations to help you master certain embroidery stitches used in the book.

I hope you have as much fun creating your own special toys as I did designing them.

Basic information

KNITTED FABRICS

All knitted fabrics are made using just two basic stitches, knit and purl.

GARTER STITCH (g st)

This is often referred to as plain knitting because every row is made with the same stitch, either knit or purl. This produces a reversible fabric with raised horizontal ridges on both sides of the work. It is looser than stockinette stitch. One of the advantages of garter stitch is that it does not curl.

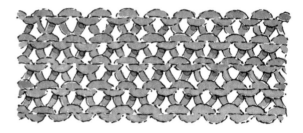

STOCKINETTE STITCH (st st)

The most widely used knitted fabric. Alternate knit rows with purl rows. With the knit side as the right side it makes a flat, smooth surface that tends to curl at the edges. It needs finishing with bands, borders, or hems.

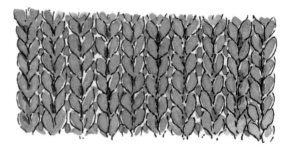

SINGLE RIB

Single rib is formed by alternating knit and purl stitches on each row to form columns of stitches. It produces an elastic fabric which is ideal for borders and neckbands. It is generally knitted on a smaller needle than the main fabric to keep it firm.

For an even number of stitches the pattern will be as follows:

*k1, p1, rep from * to end

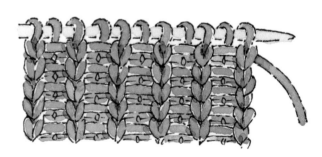

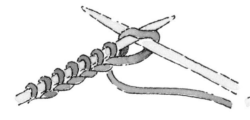

1 Knit the first stitch.

2 Bring the yarn through the needles to the front of the work and purl the next stitch.

3 Take the yarn through the needles to the back of the work and knit the next stitch.

Repeat steps 2 and 3 until all the stitches are on the right needle, ending with a purl stitch.

Turn the work and start again from step 1.

SEED STITCH

This is a basic textured stitch. It is made up of alternating knit and purl stitches. Stitches that are knitted on one row will be purled on the next row and stitches that are purled on one row will be knitted on the following row. The fabric is firm and noncurling, as well as reversible, making it ideal for collars and cuffs.

For an odd number of stitches, the instructions will be as follows:

Patt row: K1, * p1, k1, rep from * to end.
Repeat this row.

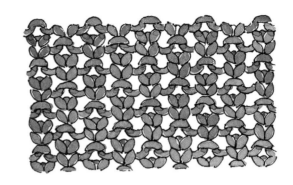

GAUGE

Obtaining the correct gauge is extremely important. It controls both the shape and size of an article, so any variations, however slight, can distort the finished look of the item. A tighter or looser gauge will produce a smaller or larger toy than that shown in the photograph and if the gauge is particularly loose, you may find that you have a very open fabric through which stuffing will show. Before starting a project, you are advised to knit a square in pattern and/or stockinette stitch (depending on the pattern instruction) of perhaps 5–10 more stitches and 5–10 more rows than those given in the gauge note. Place the finished square on a flat surface and measure the central area. If you have too many stitches to 4 in. (10 cm), try again using larger needles; if you have too few stitches to 4 in. (10 cm), try again using smaller needles. Once you have achieved the correct gauge your garment will be knitted to the measurements given at the beginning of each pattern.

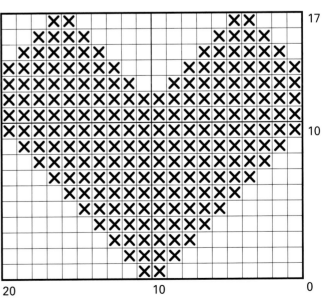

CHART NOTE

Some of the patterns in the book have charts. Each square on a chart represents a stitch and each line of squares a row of knitting. When working from the charts, read odd rows (K) from right to left and the even rows (P) from left to right, unless otherwise stated. Each color used is given a different symbol or letter and these are shown in the key alongside the chart of each pattern.

☐ color 1
☒ color 2

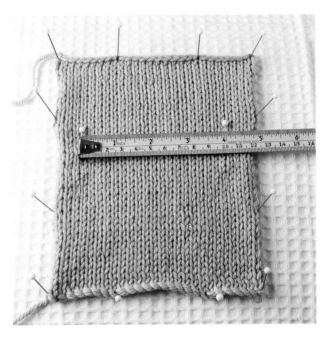

CHANGING COLOR

There are two main methods of working color into a knitted fabric: intarsia and Fair Isle techniques, but the projects in this book only use the first method. This produces a single thickness of fabric and is usually used where a color is only required in a particular area of a row and does not form a repeating pattern across the row. The simplest way to do intarsia is to cut short lengths of yarn for each motif or block of color used in a row. Then, joining in the various colors at the appropriate point on the row, link one color to the next by twisting them around each other where they meet on the wrong side to avoid gaps. All ends can then either be darned along the color join lines, as each motif is completed, or can be "knitted-in" to the fabric of the knitting as each color is worked into the pattern. It is essential that the gauge is noted for intarsia as this may vary from the stockinette stitch if both are used in the same pattern.

PRESSING

Take a little time to press finished pieces before stitching them together, as this will help to match the edges accurately. After darning in all the ends, block each piece, except ribs, gently, using a warm iron over a damp cloth. Take special care to press the edges as this will make the sewing up both easier and neater. After sewing up, press seams and hems. Ribbed welts and neckbands and any areas of garter stitch should not be pressed.

FINISHING INSTRUCTIONS

When stitching the pieces together, match the color patterns very carefully. Use a back stitch for all main knitting seams and an edge-to-edge stitch for all ribs unless otherwise stated.

EMBROIDERY STITCHES

FRENCH KNOT

Bring needle and thread out at the required position (A). Wind yarn around needle twice. Turn, pulling twists lightly against needle. Insert right next to the hole from which it emerged. Pull yarn through to back.

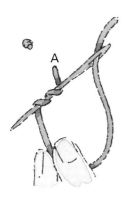
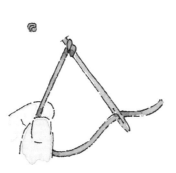

STEM STITCH

Bring needle out at A. Insert at B and emerge at C [half way between A and B]. Continue in this way, making short, slightly angled overlapping stitches from left to right.

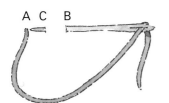
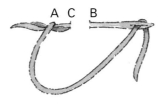

CHAIN STITCH

Bring the needle out at A, insert at A and emerge at B, looping yarn under tip of needle. Pull yarn through to make the first loop. Continue in this way.

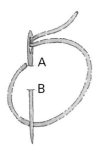

SATIN STITCH

Bring the needle out at A. Work stitches close together. Stitches can be made straight across or at an angle depending on the required finish. Care must be taken to keep a good edge, do not pull thread too tightly, or the knitting will be distorted.

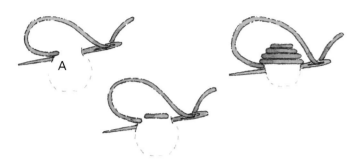

LAZY DAISY STITCH

Bring needle out at A. Insert at A, and emerge at B, looping yarn under tip of needle. Pull needle through and over loop and insert at C. Emerge at D for next stitch.

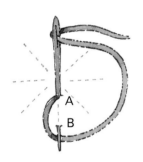

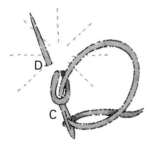

STAR STITCH

Bring needle out at A. Insert at B, and emerge at C, Insert needle at D, emerge at E, insert needle at F, thus completing the stitch.

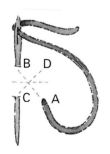

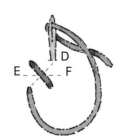

ADDITIONAL TECHNIQUES

CORDING

Cut the required number of strands of yarn 2 to 3 times the length of the finished cord. Knot together at each end and attach one end to a hook. Insert a knitting needle through the other end and turn clockwise until the strands are tightly twisted. Holding the cord in the center, bring the two ends together so that the two halves twist together. Knot the cut ends together and trim.

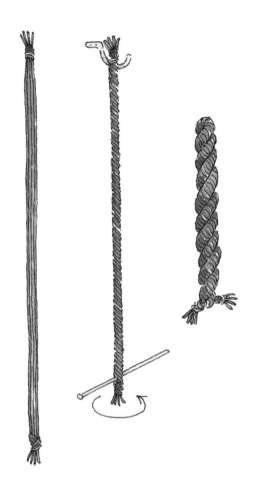

FRINGE

Cut the yarn into the required lengths. With the wrong side of the fabric facing you, insert a crochet hook from the front to the back, fold two strands in half and place the loop on the hook. Pull the loop of yarn through, then draw the ends through this loop and pull the knot tight. Repeat at regular intervals.

KNITTING NEEDLE CONVERSION TABLE

Metric	American	British
2 mm	-	14
2¼ mm	1	13
2¾ mm	2	12
3 mm	-	11
3¼ mm	3	10
3½ mm	4	-
3¾ mm	5	9
4 mm	6	8
4½ mm	7	7
5 mm	8	6
5½ mm	9	5
6 mm	10	4
6½ mm	-	3
7 mm	10½	2
7½ mm	-	1
8 mm	11	0
9 mm	13	00
10 mm	15	000

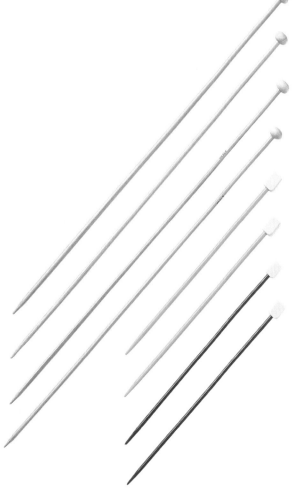

GLOSSARY OF UK/US TERMS

cast off = bind off
color = shade
knit up = pick up and knit
make up (garment) = finish (garment)
moss stitch = seed stitch
st st = stockinette st
tension = gauge
yarn forward, yarn over needle or yarn round
needle = yarn over

ABBREVIATIONS

alt	alternate
beg	begin(ning)
cont	continue
ch	chain stitch (crochet)
dc	double crochet
dec	decreas(e)(ing)
EOR	every other row
foll	following
g st	garter stitch (k every row)
inc	increas(e)(ing)
k	knit
m1	make one by raised increasing
mm	millimeters
meas	measures
patt	pattern
p	purl
psso	pass slipped stitch over
rem	remain(ing)
rep	repeat
rev st st	reverse stockinette stitch (RS row p, WS row k)
RS	right side
skp	slip 1, knit 1, pass slipped stitch over
sl 1	slip one stitch
st(s)	stitch(es)
st st	stockinette stitch (RS row k, WS row p)
tbl	through back of loop(s)
tog	together
WS	wrong side
yb	yarn back
yfwd	yarn forward
yon	yarn over needle
yrn	yarn round needle

YARNS

Patons Diploma Gold DK: a double-knitting yarn (55% wool, 25% acrylic, 20% nylon); approximately 131 yd/120 m per 1¾ oz/50 g ball.

Patons Diploma Gold 4 Ply: a sport weight yarn (55% wool, 25% acrylic, 20% nylon); approximately 201 yd/184 m per 1¾ oz/50 g ball.

Rowan Handknit DK Cotton: a medium-weight cotton yarn (100% cotton); approximately 90 yd/85 m per 1¾ oz/50 g ball.

Rowan 4 Ply Cotton: a sport weight cotton yarn (100% cotton); approximately 182 yd/170 m per 1¾ oz/50 g ball.

Rowan 4 Ply Soft: a sport weight yarn (100% merino wool); aproximately 186 yd/175 m per 1¾ oz/50 g ball.

Rowan Kid Classic: a 70% lambswool, 26% kid mohair, 4% nylon yarn, approximately 151 yd/140 m per 1¾ oz/50 g ball.

Rowan Kidsilk Haze: a 70% super kid mohair, 30% silk yarn, approximately 229 yd/210 m per 1 oz/25 g ball.

Rowan Lurex Shimmer: an 80% rayon, 20% polyester yarn, approximately 103 yd/95 m per 1 oz/25 g ball.

Jaeger Baby Merino DK: a double-knitting yarn (100% merino); approximately 131 yd/120 m per 1¾ oz/50 g ball.

Jaeger Matchmaker Merino DK: a double-knitting wool yarn (100% merino wool); approximately 131 yd/120 m per 1¾ oz/50 g ball.

Jaeger Matchmaker Merino 4 Ply: a sport weight yarn (100% merino wool); approximately 200 yd/183 m per 1¾ oz/50 g ball.

Jaeger Luxury Tweed: a sport weight yarn (100% merino wool); approximately 199 yd/180 m per 1¾ oz/50 g ball.

Jaeger Shetland: a chunky yarn (80% wool, 20% alpaca); approximately 171 yd/166 m per 3½ oz/100 g ball.

CARE INSTRUCTIONS

Check on ball band for washing instructions.

STUFFING

Always use washable toy stuffing that conforms to safety standards for toy projects. Take care not to overstuff the toys as the fabric may stretch so that the stuffing shows through; likewise, understuffing can make the toy too limp.

SAFETY

When knitting toys for children, it is important to bear in mind the age of the child for whom it is intended. Never use buttons or plastic notions for eyes as they could easily come loose and be swallowed. In general, make sure that toys given to young children have all notions securely attached and sewn in place.

Ball with bell

This delightful ball is perfect for a newborn baby – the combination of bright colors, soft yarn, and a gently tinkling bell sewn inside means it will provide lots of stimulation.

MEASUREMENTS
Height of ball approximately 5 in. (12 cm)

MATERIALS
• Small amounts of Rowan Handknit DK Cotton (50 g balls) in Sunflower (A), Flame (B), Rosso (C), Diana (D), Oasis (E) and Gooseberry (F)
or
• Small amounts in Popcorn (A), Lupin (B), Flame (C), Gooseberry (D), Ice Water (E) and Pink (F)
• Pair of 3 (3¼ mm) knitting needles
• 1 toy bell
• Washable toy stuffing

ABBREVIATIONS
See page 14.

GAUGE
24 sts and 32 rows to 4 in. (10 cm) measured over stockinette stitch using 3 (3¼ mm) needles.

FIRST SECTION
With 3 (3¼ mm) needles and A, cast on 1 st.
Knit into back and front of this st. (2 sts.)
Cont in A, work in st st, starting with a p row.
Inc into first and last st on next 2 rows.
Inc into first and last st on EOR twice.
Inc into first and last st every 3rd row, twice. (14 sts.)
Work 3 rows even.
Inc into first and last st on next row. (16 sts.)
Work 16 rows even.
Dec 1 st at each end of next row. (14 sts.)
Work 5 rows even.
Dec 1 st at each end of every 3rd row, twice. (10 sts.)
Work 3 rows even.
Dec 1 st at each end of EOR twice.
Dec 1 st at each end of next 2 rows.
P 1 row. K2tog, and fasten off.
Repeat to make 5 more sections in the same way using colors B, C, D, E, F.

FINISHING
Join sections neatly, leaving a small opening.
Insert the stuffing and bell and sew up the opening.

Penguin

Penguins are universally adored by children and adults alike. Who could resist this cuddly knitted version? The simple design means that he is perfect for a beginner knitter.

MEASUREMENTS
9 in. (23 cm) tall

MATERIALS
- 1 x 50 g ball Patons Diploma Gold DK in Black (MC)
- Small amounts of White (A), Yellow (B), Orange (C) and Blue (D)
- Washable toy stuffing
- Pair of 3 (3¼ mm) knitting needles

ABBREVIATIONS
See page 14.

GAUGE
24 sts and 32 rows to 4 in. (10 cm) measured over stockinette stitch using 3 (3¼ mm) needles.

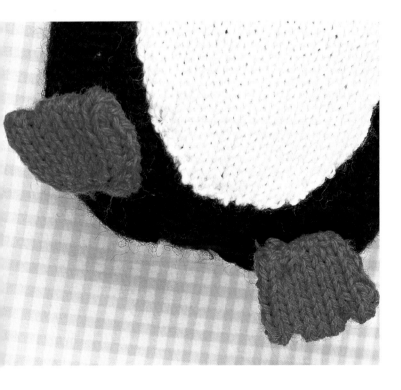

BODY
With 3 (3¼ mm) needles and MC, cast on 20 sts.
1st row: [WS] Purl to end.
2nd row: [RS] Inc in each st to end. (40 sts.)
Rep these 2 rows, once more. (80 sts.)
Cont even until work meas 7 in. (18 cm), ending with a WS row.
Next row: [RS] [K2tog] to end. (40 sts.)
Work 11 rows st st.
Next row: [RS] [K2tog] to end. (20 sts.) P 1 row. Rep last 2 rows once more. (10 sts.)
Break yarn, thread through rem sts, pull up and fasten off securely.

CHEST
With 3 (3¼ mm) needles and A, cast on 10 sts.
Work in st st and inc 1 st at each end of next 7 rows. (24 sts.)
Cont even until work measures 4 in. (10 cm).
Cont in st st, at the same time dec 1 st at each end of next 7 rows. (10 sts.) Bind off rem 10 sts.

FLIPPERS (make 2)
With 3 (3¼ mm) needles and MC, cast on 7 sts.
Work in g st and inc 1 st at each end of next 5 rows. (17 sts.)
Cont even for 2½ in. (6 cm).
Dec 1 st at each end of next 5 rows. (7 sts.)
Bind off.

FLIPPER LININGS (make 2)
With 3 (3¼ mm) needles and A, cast on 5 sts.
Work in st st and inc 1 st at each end of next 4 rows. (13 sts.)
Cont straight for 2 in. (5.5 cm).
Dec 1 st at each end of next 4 rows. (5 sts.)
Bind off.
Sew each pair of flippers together, placing white on the inside of the black.

FEET (make 2)

With 3 (3¼ mm) needles and C, cast on 5 sts.
Next row: Inc in every st. (10 sts.)
Work in st st for 9 rows.
Next row: K1, [k2, yo, k2tog] twice, k1. (10 sts.)
Beg with a p row, work 8 rows in st st.
Next row: [P2tog] to end. (5 sts.) Bind off.
Fold in half, sew cast-on and bind-off edges together.

BEAK

With 3 (3¼ mm) needles and B, cast on 12 sts.
Work in st st and dec 1 st at each end of EOR 5 times.
(2 sts.)
K2tog. Fasten off.

FINISHING

Join body seam neatly, and stuff firmly.
Fold wings in half and attach, with white side
positioned next to body.
Slip stitch chest in position centrally on the front of
penguin.
Embroider eyes with Blue in satin stitch as shown in
photograph.
Join seam of beak, and attach to face, position
between eyes and just below.
Sew feet to front of base, position with a gap in
between.

Duck

This lovely duck will make a superb companion and is quite at home perched at the end of a bed or on a windowsill. The bright colors will appeal to younger children.

SKILL LEVEL 1

MEASUREMENTS
8½ in. (22 cm) tall when seated

MATERIALS
- 1 x 50 g ball Patons Diploma Gold DK in Yellow (MC)
- Small amounts of Orange (A) and Black (B)
- Washable toy stuffing
- Polystyrene granules
- Pair of 3 (3 mm) knitting needles

ABBREVIATIONS
See page 14.

TENSION
26 sts and 36 rows to 4 in. (10 cm) measured over stockinette stitch using 3 (3 mm) needles.
26 sts and 42 rows to 4 in. (10 cm) measured over garter stitch using 3 (3 mm) needles.

BODY BACK
With 3 (3 mm) needles and MC, cast on 46 sts.
1st row: [RS] Knit to end.
2nd row: [WS] Purl to end.
Work in st st for 30 rows.
Dec 1 st at each end of next row, then EOR until 30 sts rem.
Dec 1 st at each end of every row until 20 sts rem.
Bind off.

BODY FRONT
With 3 (3 mm) needles and MC, cast on 36 sts.
1st row: [RS] Knit to end.
2nd row: [WS] Purl to end.
Work in st st for 30 rows.
Dec 1 st at each end of next row, then every 3rd row until 28 sts rem.
Dec 1 st at each end of 3rd row, then EOR until

20 sts rem.
Work 1 row. Bind off.

BASE
With 3 (3 mm) needles and MC, cast on 36 sts.
Work in st st for 10 rows.
Dec 1 st at each end of next row.
Work 4 rows, dec 1 st at each end of next row.
Dec 1 st at each end EOR 3 times.
Dec 1 st at each end of every row until there are 18 sts. Bind off.

HEAD
With 3 (3 mm) needles and MC, cast on 30 sts.
1st row: [RS] Knit to end.
2nd row: [WS] Purl to end.
Next row: [Inc 1, k1] to end. (45 sts.)
P 1 row.

Next row: [K1, inc 1, k1] to end. (60 sts.)
Work in st st for 3 rows.
Next row: [K1, inc 1, k2] to end. (75 sts.)
Work in st st for 11 rows.
Shape face
Next row: K15, [k2tog, k1] 3 times, k27, [k2tog, k1] 3 times, k15. (69 sts.)
Work 1 row.
Next row: K15, [k2tog] 3 times, k27, [k2tog] 3 times, k15. (63 sts.)
Work in st st for 9 rows.
Next row: [K1, k2tog] to end. (42 sts.)
Next row: [K1, k2tog] to end. (28 sts.)
Next row: [K2tog] to end. (14 sts.)
Break yarn, thread through rem sts, pull up and fasten off securely.

ARMS [make 4]
With 3 (3 mm) needles and MC, cast on 10 sts.
1st row: [RS] Knit to end.
2nd row: [WS] Purl to end. Working in st st throughout, inc 1 st at each end of every row until there are 16 sts.
Work even for 2 rows.
Inc 1 st at each end of next row.
Work 5 rows.
Dec 1 st at each end EOR until there are 10 sts.
Work even for 22 rows.
Bind off rem sts.

LEGS [make 2]
With 3 (3 mm) needles and A, cast on 20 sts.
Work in g st until work meas 3½ in. (9 cm).
Bind off.

FEET [make 4]
With 3 (3 mm) needles and A, cast on 10 sts.
Work in g st throughout. Inc 1 st at each end of every 3rd row until there are 24 sts.

Shape Front
Next row: K8, turn and work on these sts only. Dec 1 st at each end on next row, then EOR once. (4 sts.)
Work 1 row.
Bind off.
Rejoin yarn to rem 16 sts.
K8. Turn and work on these sts only.
Dec 1 st at each end on next row, then EOR once. (4 sts.)
Work 1 row. Bind off.
Rejoin yarn to rem 8 sts.
K 1 row.
Dec 1 st at each end of next row, then EOR once. (4 sts.)
Work 1 row.
Bind off off.

BEAK [make 2]
With 3 (3 mm) needles and A, cast on 8 sts.
Work in g st throughout.
Next row: Inc 1 st, k to end.
Rep last row until there are 18 sts. Work 8 rows even.
Bind off.

FINISHING
Join each leg seam.
Sew feet pieces together, leaving top edge open.
Stuff legs and feet quite firmly with toy stuffing.
Sew cast-on edges of legs on to center of foot.
Sew bind-off edges of legs to body, leaving a gap of 1½ in. (4 cm) in between.
Join body seam neatly leaving neck edge open.
Stuff body with toy stuffing.
Join head seam, leaving neck edge open, then stuff firmly with toy stuffing.
Place head and body seams together, and join together along neck edge.
The head seam runs down center back.
Join arms pieces together.
Leaving top edge open, fill lightly with polystyrene granules.
Position arms to top of body side seams as shown on photograph.
Join beak pieces, leaving top edge open and stuff firmly with toy stuffing.
Position and attach to face.
Embroider eyes in Black using satin stitch. Make sure they are evenly spaced above the beak.

Bugs

These charming knitted bugs with their smiling faces are
perfect for hanging over a stroller or crib. Alternatively, you
could make them into a mobile for the nursery.

SKILL LEVEL 1

MEASUREMENTS
2¼ in. (6 cm) long

MATERIALS
• Scraps of Patons Diploma Gold 4 ply in Black,
  Yellow, Green, Pink, Red, Blue, Violet.
• Small amount washable toy stuffing
• Pair of 2 (2¾ mm) knitting needles

ABBREVIATIONS
See page 14.

GAUGE
30 sts and 38 rows to 4 in. (10 cm) measured over
stockinette stitch using 2 (2¾ mm) needles.

BEE
BODY
With 2 (2¾ mm) needles and Black, cast on 6 sts.
Next row: Inc in each st knitwise. (12 sts.)
Next row: Inc in each st purlwise. (24 sts.)
Join in Yellow, working in stripes of 2 rows Yellow,
2 rows Black, cont as follows:
1st row: Knit to end.
2nd row: K1, p22, k1.
Rep these last 2 rows 8 more times. (18 rows.)
Break off Black and join in Pink.
Work 8 rows st st.
Next row: [K2tog] to end. (12 sts.)
Next row: [P2tog] to end. (6 sts.)
Break yarn, thread through rem sts, pull up tightly
and fasten off securely.

LEGS (make 6)
With 2 (2¾mm) needles and Black, cast on 4 sts and
work in st st for 10 rows. Bind off.

ANTENNAE (make 2)
**With 2 (2¾ mm) needles and Yellow, cast on 1 st.
Make bobble as follows:
[k1, p1, k1] into next st, turn, p3, turn, k3, turn, p3tog,
pull up and fasten off, forming a bobble. **
***With black, cast on 4 sts. Work 4 rows st st.
Bind off.
Roll up from cast-on edge to bind-off edge and stitch
along edge.
Sew bobble in place to top of antenna.***

WINGS (make 2)
With 2 (2¾ mm) needles and Black, cast on 5 sts.
Next row: Inc in every st. (10 sts.)
Knit every row for 15 rows.
Break yarn, thread through rem sts, pull up tightly
and fasten off securely.

FINISHING
Join body seam neatly, leaving a small opening. Stuff
body, then stitch up small opening.
Sew the gathered edges of wings to the top of the
body as in photograph.
With Black, make a tightly twisted cord loop (see
page 13) and stitch in between the wings.
Stitch side seams of legs and stitch to under side of
body.
Work a few satin stitches in Red for nose, French knot
in Black for eyes, stem stitch in Black for mouth.
Attach the antennae behind the eyes.

BLUE BUG

BODY

With 2 (2¾mm) needles and Blue, cast on 6 sts.

Next row: Inc in each st knitwise. (12 sts.)

Next row: Inc in each st purlwise. (24 sts.)

Work 2 rows Blue, then join in Violet, working in stripes as follows:

2 rows Violet, 4 rows Blue.

1st row: Knit to end.

2nd row: Purl to end.

Rep these last 6 rows twice more. (18 rows.)

Work 2 rows Violet.

Break off Violet, and join in Pink.

Work 8 rows st st.

Next row: [K2tog] to end. (12 sts.)

Next row: [P2tog] to end. (6 sts.)

Break yarn, thread through rem sts, pull up tightly and fasten off securely.

LEGS (make 6)

With 2 (2¾mm) needles and Violet, cast on 4 sts and work in st st for 10 rows. Bind off.

ANTENNAE (make 2)

With Violet, make bobble as for Bee from ** to **.

With Blue, make antennae as for Bee from *** to ***.

WINGS

With Violet, work as for Bee wings.

FINISHING

With Violet, make cord, and complete finishing as for Bee.

LADYBUG

BODY

With 2 (2¾ mm) needles and Red, cast on 6 sts.

Next row: Inc in each st knitwise. (12 sts.)

Next row: Inc in each st purlwise. (24 sts.)

Work in st st for 18 rows.

Break off Red, and join in Pink.

Work 8 rows st st.

Next row: [K2tog] to end. (12 sts.)

Next row: [P2tog] to end. (6 sts.)

Break yarn, thread through rem sts, pull up tightly and fasten off securely.

For legs, wings and cord work as for Bee.

ANTENNAE (make 2)
With Red, make bobble as for Bee from ** to **.
With Black, make antennae as for Bee from *** to
***.

FINISHING
With Black, satin stitch black spots on red body.
Complete finishing as for Bee.

GREENFLY
BODY
With 2 (2¾ mm) needles and Green, cast on 6 sts.
Next row: Inc in each st knitwise. (12 sts.)
Next row: Inc in each st purlwise. (24 sts.)
Work 2 rows Green, then join in Violet, working in
stripes as follows:
4 rows Violet, 4 rows Green.
Rep these last 8 rows twice. (16 rows.)
Break off Green. Join in Pink, work 8 rows st st.
Next row: [K2tog] to end. (12 sts.)
Next row: [P2tog] to end. (6 sts.)

△ *Thread the bugs on to a length of yarn to hang over a stroller.*

Break yarn, thread through rem sts, pull up tightly
and fasten off securely.

LEGS (make 6)
With 2 (2¾ mm) needles and Green, cast on 4 sts and
work in st st for 10 rows. Bind off.

ANTENNAE (make 2)
With Yellow, make bobble as for Bee from ** to **.
With Green, make antennae as for Bee from *** to
***.

WINGS
With Green, work as for Bee wings.

FINISHING
With Green, make cord, and complete finishing as
for Bee.

Farm animal finger puppets

Children love farmyard animals and these delightful finger puppets will provide endless amusement. Choose from a rabbit, cow, pig, mouse, or lamb – or knit the whole set!

SKILL LEVEL 1

MEASUREMENTS
3 in. (8 cm) tall

MATERIALS
- Scraps of Jaeger Matchmaker Merino 4 ply in White (A), Black (B), Oatmeal (C), Pink (D), and Gray (E).
- Scraps of Jaeger Luxury Tweed in Pebble (F)
- Scraps of dark pink embroidery thread
- Small amount washable toy stuffing
- Pair of 2 (2¾ mm) knitting needles
- Pair of 2 (2¾ mm) double pointed knitting needles

ABBREVIATIONS
See page 14.

GAUGE
30 sts and 38 rows to 4 in. (10 cm) measured over stockinette stitch using 2 (2¾ mm) needles.

△ Rabbit finger puppet

RABBIT
BODY AND HEAD
With 2 (2¾ mm) needles and E, cast on 20 sts.
Knit 2 rows.
**1st row: Knit.
2nd row: Purl.
Cont in st st until 12 rows have been worked.
Shape head
13th row: [K2tog, k1] 6 times, k2tog. (13 sts.)
14th row: Purl.
15th row: K1, inc 1 st in every st to end. (25 sts.)
Work in st st for 9 rows.
25th row: [K1, k2tog] 8 times, k1. (17 sts.)

26th row: Purl.
27th row: [K2tog, k1] 5 times, k2tog. (11 sts.)
Next row: [P2tog, p1] 3 times, p2tog. (7 sts.)
Break yarn, thread through rem sts, pull up tightly and fasten off securely. Sew seam.**

OUTER EARS [make 2]
With 2 (2¾ mm) needles and E, cast on 6 sts.
Work in g st for 10 rows.
11th row: K2tog, k2, k2tog. (4 sts.)
Cont in g st for 3 rows.
15th row: [K2tog] twice. (2 sts.)
16th row: K2tog. Fasten off.

INNER EARS [make 2]

With 2 (2¾ mm) needles and D, cast on 5 sts.
Work in st st for 10 rows.
11th row: Sl 1, k1, psso, k1, k2tog.
Work 3 rows.
15th row: Sl 1, k2tog, psso. Fasten off.
With WS of inner ear to outer ear, sew inner ear in
place. Make tuck in cast-on edge and sew cast-on
edges to head.

PAWS [make 2]

With 2 (2¾ mm) double-pointed needles and E, cast
on 8 sts.
1st row: K8, *do not turn, slide sts to opposite end of
needle and take yarn tightly across back of work,
knit 8 sts again, rep from * 4 more times, change to
A, work 2 more rows, do not turn, slide sts to
opposite end of needle and take yarn tightly across
back of work, [k2tog] 4 times, do not turn, slide sts to
opposite end of needle and take yarn tightly across
back of work, sl 1, k3tog, psso and fasten off. Insert
small amount of toy stuffing into paw, and then sew
cast-on end to body.

FINISHING

Make small pompon using A and sew to back for tail.
Using Black, embroider French knots for eyes and
straight stitches for nose and mouth.

COW

BODY AND HEAD

Using A, work as for Body and Head of Rabbit.
Break yarn, thread through rem sts, pull up tightly
and fasten off securely. Sew seam.

EARS [make 1 in A, 1 in B]

With 2 (2¾ mm) needles, cast on 5 sts.
Work in g st for 8 rows.
5th row: K2tog, k1, k2tog. (3 sts.)
6th row: K3.
7th row: Sl 1, k2tog, psso. (1 st.)
Fasten off.
Fold sides of each ear at cast-on edges and attach to
head.

HORNS [make 2]

With 2 (2¾ mm) needles and C, cast on 3 sts. Work in
st st for 3 rows.
Next row: K3tog.
Fasten off. Attach horns to top of head between ears.

△ *Cow finger puppet*

LEGS [make 2]

With 2 (2¾ mm) double-pointed needles and A, cast
on 8 sts.
1st row: K8, *do not turn, slide sts to opposite end of
needle and take yarn tightly across back of work, knit
8 sts again, rep from * 4 more times, change to C,
work 2 more rows, do not turn, slide sts to opposite
end of needle and take yarn tightly across back of
work, [k2tog] 4 times, do not turn, slide sts to
opposite end of needle and take yarn tightly across
back of work, sl 1, k3tog, psso and fasten off. Insert
small amount of toy stuffing into paw, and then sew
cast-on end to body. Make second leg, using B in
place of A.

TAIL

With A, make a twisted cord, approx ¾ in. (2 cm)
long.
With B, make a tassle, and attach to one end of tail.
Sew other end of tail to body.

MUZZLE

With 2 (2¾ mm) needles and C, cast on 3 sts.
Beg with a p row, work in st st at the same time inc
1 st at each end of next row. (5 sts.)
Next row: Inc 1 st, knit to last st, inc 1 st. (7 sts.)
Work 2 rows.
Next row: Dec 1 st, p to last st, dec 1 st. (5 sts.)

Next row: Dec 1 st, k to last st, dec 1 st. (3 sts.)
Bind off.

PATCH [make 1]
With 2 (2¾ mm) needles and B, cast on 3 sts.
Beg with a K row, work in st st, inc 1 st at each end of
next row, then EOR once. (7 sts.)
Work 2 rows even. Dec 1 st at each end of next row,
then EOR once. (3 sts.) Bind off.

FINISHING
Sew on muzzle. Using Black, embroider French knots
for eyes and nostrils, and stem stitch for mouth.

PIG
BODY AND HEAD
With 2 (2¾ mm) needles and D, cast on 20 sts.
Knit 2 rows.
**1st row: Knit.
2nd row: Purl.
Cont in st st until 12 rows have been worked.
Shape head
13th row: [K2tog, k1] 6 times, k2tog. (13 sts.)
14th row: Purl.
15th row: K1, inc 1 st in every st to end. (25 sts.)
Work in st st for 9 rows.
25th row: [K1, k2tog] 8 times, k1. (17 sts.)
26th row: Purl.
27th row: [K2tog, k1] 5 times, k2tog. (11 sts.)
Next row: [P2tog, p1] 3 times, p2tog. (7 sts.)
Break yarn, thread through rem sts, pull up tightly
and fasten off securely. Sew seam.**

EARS [make 2]
With 2 (2¾ mm) needles and D, cast on 5 sts.
Work in g st for 4 rows.
5th row: K2tog, k1, k2tog. (3 sts.)
6th row: K3.
7th row: Sl 1, k2tog, psso. (1 st.)
Fasten off. Sew cast-on edges of ears to sides of
head, gathering base slightly.

PAWS [make 2]
With 2 (2¾ mm) double-pointed needles and D, cast
on 8 sts.
1st row: K8, *do not turn, slide sts to opposite end of
needle and take yarn tightly across back of work, knit
8 sts again, rep from * 4 more times, change to C,
work 2 more rows, do not turn, slide sts to opposite
end of needle and take yarn tightly across back of
work, [k2tog] 4 times, do not turn, slide sts to

opposite end of needle and take yarn tightly across
back of work.
Sl 1, k3tog, psso and fasten off. Insert small amount
of toy stuffing into paw, and then sew cast-on end to
body.

SNOUT [make 1]
With 2 (2¾ mm) needles and C, cast on 4 sts.
Beg with a p row, work 7 rows in st st, inc 1 st at each
end of 2nd row, then EOR once. (8 sts.)
8th row: K2tog, k4, k2tog. (6 sts.)
9th row: P6.
10th row: K2tog, k2, k2tog. (4 sts.)
Bind off rem 4 sts. Run gathering thread around
outer edge and pull up to form a snout.
Sew snout to front of head.

TAIL
With 2 (2¾ mm) needles and D, cast on 7 sts.
Work 2 rows knit. Bind off.

FINISHING
Sew on snout.
Embroider French knots for eyes using Black, and
nostrils using Dark Pink. Embroider mouth using
stem stitch.
Stuff head lightly, stitch below head shaping and
fasten to enclose stuffing.

▷ *Pig finger puppet*

MOUSE
BODY AND HEAD
Work in st st stripes as follows:
Work 2 rows B, 2 rows A.
Work as for Body and Head of Pig, working Head using A only.

OUTER EARS [make 2]
With 2 (2¾ mm) needles and A, cast on 5 sts.
Work in g st for 4 rows.
5th row: K2tog, k1, k2tog. (3 sts.)
6th row: Knit.
7th row: Sl 1, k2tog, psso. Fasten off.

INNER EARS [make 2]
With B, work as for Outer Ears. Sew ears together, leaving cast-on edge open. Turn RS out, make tuck in cast-on edge and sew to head.

PAWS [make 2]
With 2 (2¾ mm) needles and B, work as for Paws of Bunny [working stripe pattern as established].
Insert small amount of toy stuffing into paw, and then sew cast-on end to body.

▽ *Mouse finger puppet*

TAIL
With 2 (2¾ mm) double-pointed needles and B, cast on 4 sts.
1st row: K4, *do not turn, slide sts to opposite end of needle and take yarn tightly across back of work, knit 4 sts again, rep from * for 3¼ in. (8 cm), do not turn, slide sts to opposite end of needle and take yarn tightly across back of work, (k2tog) twice, do not turn, slide stitches to opposite end of needle and take yarn across back, k2tog, fasten off. Sew in place.

FINISHING
Using Black, embroider French knots for eyes, satin stitch for nose and straight stitches for mouth.

△ *Lamb finger puppet*

LAMB

BODY AND HEAD

With 2 (2¾ mm) needles and F, cast on 20 sts.
Cont in g st until 16 rows have been worked.

Shape head

13th row: [K2tog, k1] 6 times, k2tog. (13 sts.)
14th row: Knit.
15th row: K1, inc 1 st in every st to end. (25 sts.)
16th row: K11F, p3A, k11F.
17th row: K11F, K3A, k11F.
18th row: K10F, p5A, k10F.
19th row: K10F, k5A, k10F.
Rep last 2 rows once more, then 18th row again.
23rd row: With F, knit.
24th row: With F, knit.
25th row: [K1, k2tog] 8 times. K1. (17 sts.)
26th row: Knit.
27th row: [K2tog, k1] 5 times, k2tog. (11 sts.)
Next row: [K2tog, k1] 3 times, k2tog. (7 sts.)
Break yarn, thread through rem sts, pull up tightly and fasten off securely. Sew seam.

EARS (make 2)

With 2 (2¾ mm) needles and C, cast on 7 sts.
Work in g st for 6 rows.
7th row: K2tog, k3, k2tog. (5 sts.)

8th row: K2tog, k1, k2tog. (3 sts.)
Bind off rem sts.
Sew cast-on edges of ears to sides of head, gathering base slightly.

LEGS (make 2)

With 2 (2¾ mm) double-pointed needles and F, cast on 8 sts.
1st row: Seed st 8 sts, *do not turn, slide sts to opposite end of needle and take yarn tightly across back of work, seed st 8 sts again, rep from * 4 more times, change to C, work 2 rows in st st, cont in st st, do not turn, slide sts to opposite end of needle and take yarn tightly across back of work, [k2tog] 4 times, do not turn, slide sts to opposite end of needle and take yarn tightly across back of work, sl 1, k3tog, psso and fasten off.
Insert small amount of toy stuffing into paw, and then sew cast-on end to body.

FINISHING

Using E, embroider French knots for eyes, satin stitch for nose and straight stitches for mouth.

Tropical fish

With its vibrant blocks of color and big kissing lips, who could resist this delightful tropical fish. If you really like them, why not make a whole aquarium of fish in brilliant colors – just choose your favorite shades and tones in Handknit DK Cotton.

SKILL LEVEL 1

MEASUREMENTS
9½ in. (24 cm) long

MATERIALS
- Scraps of Rowan Handknit DK Cotton in Orange (MC), Yellow (A), Blue (B), Green (C) and Red (D)
- Washable toy stuffing
- Pair of 3 (3¼ mm) knitting needles

ABBREVIATIONS
See page 14.

GAUGE
24 sts and 32 rows to 4 in. (10 cm) measured over stockinette stitch using 3 (3¼ mm) needles.

BODY
With 3 (3¼ mm) needles and MC, cast on 8 sts.
Work in st st throughout.
1st row: Knit.
2nd row: Purl.
3rd row: Cast on 2 sts, k to end.
4th row: Cast on 3 sts, p to end.
Rep last 2 rows twice more.
9th row: Rep 3rd row. (25 sts.)
10th row: Inc 1 st, p to last st, inc in last st. (27 sts.)
11th row: Inc 1 st, k to last st, inc in last st. (29 sts.)
12th row: Inc 1 st, p to last st, inc in last st with A. (31 sts.)
13th row: With A, inc 1 st, k2 A, with MC k to last st, inc in last st. (33 sts.)
14th row: With MC, inc 1 st, p to last 5 sts, with A, p to last st, inc in last st. (35 sts.)
15th row: With A, inc 1 st, k6 A, with MC k to last st, inc in last st. (37 sts.)
16th row: With MC, p to last 8 sts, with A, p to end. (37 sts.)
17th row: With A, inc 1 st, k8 A, with MC, k to end, inc in last st. (39 sts.)
18th row: With MC, p to last 10 sts, with A, p to end.
19th row: With A, inc 1 st, k10 A, with MC, k to last st, inc in last st. (41 sts.)
20th row: With MC, inc 1 st, p to last 12 sts, with A, p to last st, inc in last st. (43 sts.)
21st row: K13 A, with MC, k to end.
22nd row: With MC, p to last 13 sts, with A, p to end.
23rd row: Rep 21st row.
24th row: With MC, p2tog, p to last 12 sts, with A, p10, p2tog. (41 sts.)
25th row: With A, k2tog, k10 A, with MC, k to last 2 sts, k2tog. (39 sts.)
26th row: With MC, p to last 9 sts, with A, p7, p2tog. (38 sts.)
27th row: With A, k2tog, k6 A, with MC, k to last 2 sts, k2tog. (36 sts.)
28th row: With MC, p to last 6 sts, with A, p to end.
29th row: With A, k2tog, k4 A, with MC, k to last 2 sts, k2tog. (34 sts.)
30th row: With MC, p2tog, p to last 4 sts, with A, p2, p2tog. (32 sts.)
31st row: With A, k2tog, with MC, k to last 2 sts, k2tog. (30 sts.)
32nd row: With MC, p2tog, p to last 2 sts, k2tog. (28 sts.)
33rd row: With MC, k2tog, k to last 2 sts, k2tog. (26 sts.)
34th row: With MC, p2tog, p to last 2 sts, p2tog.

(24 sts.)

35th row: With MC, bind off 2, k to end.
36th row: With MC, bind off 3, p to end.
37th row: With MC, bind off 2, k to end.
Rep last 2 rows twice more.
Work 1 row. Bind off 7 rem sts.

TAIL [make 2]

With 3 (3¼ mm) needles and C, cast on 8 sts.
Work 4 rows in st st.
5th row: Inc 1 st at each end of row. (10 sts.)
6th row: Purl.
Rep last rows twice more. (14 sts.)
11th row: Inc 1 st, k6, turn, leave rem sts on a spare needle.
12th row: P8.
13th row: K8.
Rep last 2 rows once more.
16th row: P2tog, p to end.
17th row: K to last 2 sts, k2tog.
Rep last 2 rows twice more.
22nd row: P2tog, fasten off.
Rejoin yarn to rem sts, k to last st, inc 1 st. (8 sts.)
Next row: P8.
Next row: K8.
Rep last 2 rows once more.

Next row: P to last 2 sts, p2tog.
Next row: K2tog, k to end.
Rep last 2 rows twice more.
22nd row: P2tog, fasten off.

TOP FIN [A]

With 3 (3¼ mm) needles and B, cast on 17 sts.
1st row: Knit.
2nd row: Purl.
3rd row: Inc 1 st, k to end.
4th row: Dec 1 st, p to end.
Rep last rows twice more. (17 sts.)
9th row: Knit.
10th row: Dec 1 st, p to end. (16 sts.)
11th row: Knit.
12th row: Bind off 3, p to end. (13 sts.)
13th row: Inc 1 st, k to end. (14 sts.)
14th row: Bind off 5, p to end. (9 sts.)
15th row: Knit.
Bind off rem 9 sts.

TOP FIN [B]

With 3 (3¼ mm) needles and B, cast on 17 sts.
1st row: Purl.
2nd row: Knit.
Work fin as set for Top Fin A, reversing all shapings.

LOWER FIN [C] [make 2]

With 3 (3¼ mm) needles and D, cast on 8 sts.
1st row: Knit.
2nd row: Purl.
3rd row: Knit.
4th row: Inc 1 st, p to end. (9 sts.)
5th row: Knit.
6th row: Inc 1 st, p to end. (10 sts.)
7th row: K2tog, k to end. (9 sts.)
8th row: Purl.
9th row: Dec 1 st, k to last st, inc 1 st. (9 sts.)
10th row: P to last 2 sts, p2tog.
11th row: Dec 1 st, k to end.
Rep last 2 rows once more. (5 sts.)
14th row: Rep 10th row.
Bind off rem 4 sts.

LOWER FIN [D] [make 2]

With 3 (3¼ mm) needles and D, cast on 8 sts.
Work fin as for Lower Fin C, reversing all shapings.

LIPS [make 2]

With 3 (3¼ mm) needles and D, cast on 8 sts.
1st row: Knit.
2nd row: Purl.
3rd row: Cast on 2, k to end.
4th row: Cast on 3, p to end. (11 sts.)
Rep last 2 rows twice more. (21 sts.)
Inc 1 st at each end of next 4 rows. (29 sts.)
Bind off.

FINISHING

Using C, embroider chain stitch line across body
sections where MC and A meet.
Join body seam neatly, leaving a small opening, stuff
then stitch up small opening.
Sew tail together, sew cast-on edge to end of body.
Stitch top fins A and B together.
Sew cast-on edges to top edge of body.
Stitch lower fins C and D together.
Sew cast-on edges to lower edge of body.
Using B, embroider spots for eyes in satin stitch.
Overcast lip rows together tightly, form a "heart"
shape, then sew mouth on to front of body as shown
on photograph.

Caterpillar finger puppets

These brightly colored finger puppets will give children hours of enjoyment and are ideal for young children having fun with their own puppet shows.

MEASUREMENTS
3 in. (8 cm) tall

MATERIALS
- Scraps of Patons Diploma Gold DK in Pink (A), Apple Green (B), Yellow (C), Aqua (D), Violet (E), Orange (F) and Black (for embroidery)
- Small amount washable toy stuffing
- Pair 3 (3 mm) knitting needles

ABBREVIATIONS
See page 14.

GAUGE
28 sts and 38 rows to 4 in. (10 cm) measured over stockinette stitch using 3 (3 mm) needles.

▽ Caterpillar 1

CATERPILLAR 1
BODY AND HEAD
With 3 (3 mm) needles and A, cast on 20 sts.
Knit 2 rows.
Now work in st st stripes as follows: 2 rows A, 2 rows B.
Cont in stripes until 12 rows have been worked.
Shape head
*13th row: With B only, (k2tog, k1) 6 times, k2tog. (13 sts.)
14th row: Purl.
15th row: Inc in each st to last st, k1. (25 sts.)
Work in st st for 9 rows.
25th row: [K1, k2tog] 8 times, k1. (17 sts.)
26th row: Purl.
27th row: [K2tog, k1] 5 times, k2tog. (11 sts.)
28th row: [P2tog, p1] 3 times, p2tog. (7 sts.)

Break yarn, thread through rem sts, pull up tightly and fasten off securely. *

ANTENNAE [make 2]
Using C, work as follows:
**With 3 (3 mm) needles, cast on 1 st.
Make bobble as follows:
[K1, p1, k1] into next st, turn, k3, turn, p3, turn and sl 1, k2tog, psso. Pull up and fasten off, making into a bobble.
Make antenna
Cast on 4 sts, work 4 rows st st. Bind off.
Roll up from cast-on edge to bind-off edge and stitch along edge neatly.
Sew bobble into place to top of antenna.**

RIGHT LEGS [make 3]

Using B, work as follows:

*** With 3 (3 mm) needles, cast on 4 sts, and work in g st for 2 rows.

Bind off 2 sts, work on rem 2 sts.

K into front and back of next 2 sts. (4 sts.)

Next row: P4.

Next row: K4.

Rep last 2 rows twice more.

Next row: K4.

Bind off rem 4 sts.

Sew seam edges neatly.***

LEFT LEGS [make 3]

Using B, work as follows:

**** With 3 (3 mm) needles, cast on 4 sts, and work in g st for 2 rows.

Bind off 2 sts, work on rem 2 sts.

P into front and back of next 2 sts. (4 sts.)

Next row: K4.

Next row: P4.

Rep last 2 rows twice more.

Next row: K4.

Bind off rem 4 sts.

Sew seam edges neatly.****

FINISHING

Join seam neatly on body.

Stuff head lightly, stitch below head shaping and fasten to enclose stuffing.

Sew antennae to top of head.

Sew legs on to body.

Using Black, embroider French knots for eyes and stem stitch for mouth

Using pink, work in satin st to embroider nose.

CATERPILLAR 2

BODY AND HEAD

With 3 (3 mm) needles and F, cast on 20 sts.

Knit 2 rows.

Now work in st st stripes as follows: 4 rows F, 4 rows E, 4 rows D. (12 rows.)

Shape head

With A only, work as for Caterpillar 1, from * to *.

ANTENNAE [make 2] in F

Work as for Caterpillar 1, from ** to **.

RIGHT LEGS [make 3] 1 in B, 1 in C, 1 in E

Work as for Caterpillar 1, from *** to ***.

LEFT LEGS [make 3] 1 in B, 1 in C, 1 in E

Work as for Caterpillar 1, from **** to ****.

FINISHING

Join seam neatly on body.

Stuff head lightly, stitch below head shaping and fasten to enclose stuffing.

Sew antennae to top of head.

Sew legs on to body.

Using Black, embroider French knots for eyes and stem stitch for mouth.

Using E, embroider nose in satin stitch.

▽ *Caterpillar 2*

▷ Caterpillar 3

CATERPILLAR 3

BODY AND HEAD

With 3 (3 mm) needles and C, cast on 16 sts.

Knit 2 rows.

Now work in st st stripes as follows: 2 rows C, 2 rows F, 2 rows B, 2 rows E, 2 rows A, 2 rows D. (12 rows.)

Work shaping as follows:

Next row: With C, k1, * ml, k4; rep from * to last 3 sts, m1, k3. (20 sts.)

Next row: With C, purl.

Next row: With F, k1, * m1, k5; rep from * to last 4 sts, m1, k4. (24 sts.)

Next row: With F, purl.

Next row: With B, k1, *m1, k6; rep from * to last 5 sts, m1, k5. (28 sts.)

Next row: With B, purl.

Next row: With E, knit.

Next row: With E, purl.

Next row: With A, k1, * k2tog, k5; rep from * to last 6 sts, k2tog, k4. (24 sts.)

Next row: With A, purl.

Next row: With D, k1, * k2tog, k4; rep from * to last 5 sts, k2tog, k3. (20 sts.)

Next row: With D, purl.

Next row: With C, knit.

Next row: With C, purl.

Shape head

With F only, work as for Caterpillar 1, from * to *.

ANTENNAE [make 2] in A

Work as for Caterpillar 1, from ** to **.

RIGHT LEGS [make 3] in C

Work as for Caterpillar 1, from *** to ***.

LEFT LEGS [make 3] in C

Work as for Caterpillar 1, from **** to ****.

HAT

***** With 3 (3 mm) needles and E, cast on 25 sts.

Work in st st for 12 rows.

Shape top

13th row: [K1, k2tog] 8 times, k1. (18 sts.)

14th row: Purl.

15th row: [K2tog, k1] 6 times. (12 sts.)

Next row: [P2tog, p1] 4 times. (8 sts.)

Break yarn, thread through rem sts, pull up tightly and fasten off securely. Sew seam, reversing seam on first 4 rows. *****

FINISHING

Join seam neatly on body. Stuff head lightly, stitch below head shaping and fasten to enclose stuffing.

Sew antennae to hat.

Sew legs on to body.

Using Black, embroider French knots for eyes and stem stitch for mouth. Using A, embroider nose in satin stitch.

CATERPILLAR 4
BODY AND HEAD
With 3 (3 mm) needles and C, cast on 20 sts.

1st row: [WS] Knit.

2nd row: [RS] Purl.

Rep last 2 rows twice.

7th row: Purl.

Change to B, k 1 row.

Rep 1st to 7th row.

Change to E, k 1 row.

Rep 1st to 7th row. (23 rows.)

Shape head

With D only, work as for Caterpillar 1, from * to *.

ANTENNAE [make 2] in B
Work as for Caterpillar 1, from ** to **.

RIGHT LEGS [make 3] in A
Work as for Caterpillar 1, from *** to ***.

LEFT LEGS [make 3] in A
Work as for Caterpillar 1, from **** to ****.

FINISHING
On WS of body, slip stitch the 8 rows together; this will form 3 ridges on RS.

Join seam neatly on body.

Stuff head lightly, stitch below head shaping and fasten to enclose stuffing.

Sew antennae to top of head.

Sew legs on to body.

Using Black, embroider French knots for eyes and stem stitch for mouth.

Using A, embroider nose in satin stitch.

CATERPILLAR 5
BODY AND HEAD
With 3 (3 mm) needles and F, cast on 20 sts.

1st row: [WS] With F, knit.

2nd row: [RS] With F, purl.

3rd row: With F, knit.

4th row: With C, knit.

5th row: With C, knit.

6th row: With C, purl.

7th row: With C, knit.

With D, rep rows 4 to 7.

With E, rep rows 4 to 7.

With B, rep rows 4 to 7. (19 rows.)

Shape head

With C only, work as for Caterpillar 1, from * to *.

△ Caterpillar 4

ANTENNAE [make 2] in E
Work as for Caterpillar 1, from ** to **.

RIGHT LEGS [make 3] 1 in A, 1 in C and 1 in E
Work as for Caterpillar 1, from *** to ***.

LEFT LEGS [make 3] 1 in A, 1 in C and 1 in E
Work as for Caterpillar 1, from **** to ****.

HAT in A
Work as for Caterpillar 3, from ***** to *****.

FINISHING
Join seam neatly on body.

Stuff head lightly, stitch below head shaping and fasten to enclose stuffing.

Sew antennae to top of hat.

Sew legs on to body.

Using Black, embroider French knots for eyes and stem stitch for mouth.

Using A, embroider nose in satin stitch.

▽ *Caterpillar 5*

Fairy

This pretty little fairy with her delicate wings and golden hair is a lovely toy for a little girl's bedroom. She would also be a perfect adornment for the top of a Christmas tree.

SKILL LEVEL 1

MEASUREMENTS
Approximately 10 in. (26 cm) tall

MATERIALS
- 1 x 50 g ball of Rowan 4 ply Cotton in Pink (A)
- 1 x 50 g ball of Rowan Kidsilk Haze in White (B)
- 1 x 50 g ball of Rowan Lurex Shimmer in Pewter (C)
- Scraps of yellow, black and pink sport weight wool
- Washable toy stuffing
- Pair each of 2 (2¾ mm) and 3 (3 mm) knitting needles
- Size C (2.50 mm) crochet hook

ABBREVIATIONS
See page 14.

GAUGE
4 ply Cotton tension:
32 sts and 42 rows to 4 in. (10 cm) measured over stockinette stitch using 2 (2¾ mm) needles.
Kidsilk Haze tension:
25 sts and 34 rows to 4 in. (10 cm) measured over stockinette stitch using 3 (3 mm) needles.

FAIRY
BODY
Back and front [alike]
With 2 (2¾ mm) needles and A, cast on 20 sts.
Work in st st for 24 rows, ending with a WS row.
Shape body
Dec 1 st at each end on every row 4 times. (12 sts.)
Dec 1 st at each end EOR until 6 sts rem.
Work 1 row.
Shape head
Inc 1 st at each end on every row 3 times. (12 sts.)
Inc 1 st at each end EOR twice. (16 sts.)
Work 9 rows even.
Dec 1 st at each end on next row. (14 sts.)
Work 1 row even.
Dec 1 st at each end on next 2 rows. (10 sts.)
Bind off 2 sts at beg of next 2 rows. (6 sts.)
Bind off rem 6 sts.

LEGS AND ARMS [make 4]
With A, make twisted cord using 4 strands of yarn.
[Finished length 4 in./10 cm].

SHOES [make 2]
With 3 (3 mm) needles and C, cast on 16 sts.
Work in g st as follows:
Dec 1 st at each end EOR until 8 sts rem.
Work 2 rows. Bind off.
Fold in half, sew around edges.

HANDS [make 2]
With 2 (2¾ mm) needles and A, cast on 2 sts.
Work in g st as follows:
Inc 1 st at each end EOR until there are 6 sts.
Work even for 2 rows.
Dec 1 st at each end EOR until there are 4 sts.
Bind off.

DRESS [back and front alike]
With 3 (3 mm) needles and B, cast on 40 sts.
Work in st st throughout, at the same time dec
1 st at each end of 3rd row, then EOR twice.
(34 sts.)
Now dec 1 st at each end of every 5th row, 5 times.
(24 sts.)
Now dec 1 st at each end of every 4th row, 4 times.
(16 sts.)
Next row: Knit.
Next row: [P2tog] 8 times. (8 sts.)
Bind off rem sts.

SLEEVES [make 2]
With 3 (3 mm) needles and B, cast on 10 sts.
Work in st st throughout, at the same time dec 1 st at
each end of every 4th row, 3 times. Work 4 rows
even. (4 sts.) K2tog twice. (2 sts.)
Bind off.

WINGS
With 3 (3 mm) needles and B, cast on 8 sts.
Work in g st throughout, at the same time cast on
4 sts at beg of next 8 rows. (40 sts.)
Work 2 rows even.
Bind off 2 sts at beg of next 4 rows. (32 sts.)
K 16 sts, turn, leave rem sts on a spare needle.
Bind off 2 sts at beg of next 8 rows. Fasten off.
Rejoin yarn to 16 sts, bind off 2 sts at beg of next
8 rows. Fasten off.

form hair. Strand yarn carefully to form "curly" hair. With C, tie "hair" into pig tails.

FINISHING

Join raglan seams of dress to sleeves.
Join side and sleeve seams.
Put dress on to doll.

HEM EDGING

With size C (2.50 mm) crochet hook and C, work a row of dc along cast-on edge of dress, then work as follows:
1 dc into the first st, *ch3, skip one st, 1 dc into next st, rep from * to end. Fasten off.

NECK EDGING

Work as for hem edging.

CUFF EDGING

Work as for hem edging.

WING EDGING

Work as for hem edging. Sew wings on to back of dress.

FINISHING BODY

Place RS of front and back of body together.
Sew edges together, leaving small gap at bottom of body.
Turn the body RS out. Stuff, then sew up small gap.
Attach legs to bottom of body, with a space of ¾ in. (2 cm) apart. Sew on shoes.
Attach arms to upper part of body into side seams, ¼ in. (1 cm) down from neck. Sew on hands.
Embroider French knots for eyes and satin stitch for nose using Black. Embroider stem stitch for mouth using Pink.

HAIR

Cut 30 lengths of yellow yarn approx 10 in. (25½ cm) long. Using backstitch, stitch to center of head to

Turtle

This colorful turtle makes a lovely soft toy with its large "cushioned" shell. The turtle's hat is decorated with a lazy daisy stitch.

SKILL LEVEL 2

MEASUREMENTS
9 in. (23 cm) long

MATERIALS
- 1 x 50 g ball of Patons Diploma Gold DK in Green
- Small amounts of Red, Yellow, Orange, Violet, Bright Aqua and Blue
- Washable toy stuffing
- Pair of 3 (3 mm) knitting needles

ABBREVIATIONS
See page 14.

GAUGE
24 sts and 32 rows to 4 in. (10 cm) measured over stockinette stitch using 3 (3 mm) needles.

NOTE: Seed stitch used for turtle shell throughout.

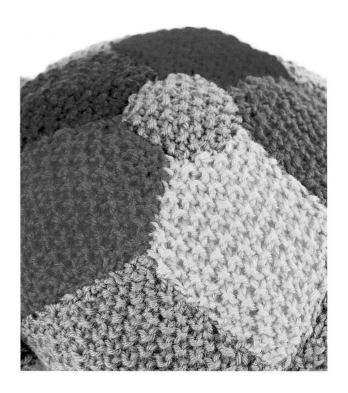

CENTER SHELL
With 3 (3 mm) needles and Green, cast on 3 sts.
1st row: K1, p1, k1.
Cont in seed st, inc 1 st at each end of next row, then EOR twice. (9 sts.)
Work 3 rows in seed st.
Dec 1 st at each end of next row, then EOR twice. (3 sts.)
Work 1 row.
Bind off.

SHELL SIDES (make 1 red, yellow, orange, violet, blue)
With 3 (3 mm) needles, cast on 3 sts.
1st row: K1, p1, k1.
Cont in seed st, inc 1 st at each end of next row, then EOR 5 times. (15 sts.)
Work 3 rows in seed st.

Cont in seed st, dec 1 st at each end of next row, then EOR 3 times. (7 sts.)
Work 1 row.
Bind off.

SHELL EDGINGS (make 5 Green)
With 3 (3 mm) needles, cast on 3 sts.
1st row: K1, p1, k1.
Cont in seed st, inc 1 st at each end of next row, then EOR 7 times. (19 sts.)
Work in seed st for 2 rows.
Bind off.

UNDERBODY (make 1)
With 3 (3 mm) needles and Green, cast on 11 sts.
Work in seed st for 1 row. Inc at each end of next row, then EOR 8 times. (29 sts.)
Cont in seed st for 28 rows.

Dec 1 st at each end of next row, then EOR 8 times. (11 sts.)
Work in seed st for 1 row. Bind off.

FEET (make 4)
With 3 (3 mm) needles and Green, cast on 18 sts.
Work 14 rows in st st. Bind off.

HEAD
With 3 (3 mm) needles and Green, cast on 20 sts.
Work 2 rows in st st.
Next row: Inc in first st, k8, inc in each of next 2 sts, k8, inc in last st. (24 sts.)
P 1 row.
Next row: Inc in first st, k10, inc in each of next 2 sts, k10, inc in last st. (28 sts.)
Work in st st for 4 rows.
Next row: K1, *k2tog, k2; rep from * to last 3 sts, k2tog, k1. (21 sts.)
Work in st st for 2 rows.
Bind off.

TAIL
With 3 (3 mm) needles and Green, cast on 10 sts.
Work 8 rows in st st.
Next row: [K2tog] 5 times. (5 sts.)
Break yarn, thread through rem sts, pull up tightly and fasten off securely.

HAT
With 3 (3 mm) needles and Blue, cast on 13 sts, work in seed st for 6 rows.
Next row: K1, (k2tog) 6 times. (7 sts.)
Break yarn, thread rem sts, pull up and fasten off securely. Sew side seam.

BRIM
With 3 (3 mm) needles and Red, cast on 30 sts.
Work in st st for 4 rows. Bind off.

FINISHING
Join shells together, green in center, blue attached to red, red to violet, violet to orange, orange to yellow. Sew shell edgings to sides of shells to complete upper section.
Stitch top to base, leaving a small gap for stuffing. Insert stuffing and close opening.
Join side and cast-on edges of legs, head and tail. Fill with stuffing and attach close to edge of shell.
Sew hat to head, inserting stuffing. Join ends of brim, then sew cast-on edge of brim to point where hat joins to head.
With Blue, embroider eyes using French knots.
With Red, embroider the mouth using stem stitch.
With Yellow, embroider flower on hat using lazy daisy stitch (see page 12). With Blue, embroider center of flower using a French knot.

Princess

This pretty princess is knitted in luxury 4 ply cotton, Kidsilk and Lurex shimmer in beautiful purples and pinks. Make your own little princess feel special with this charming toy.

SKILL LEVEL 2

MEASUREMENTS
Approximately 13 in. (33 cm) tall

MATERIALS
- 2 x 50 g balls of Rowan 4 ply Cotton in Pink (MC)
- 2 x 50 g balls of Rowan 4 ply Cotton in Mauve (B)
- Small amount of Rowan 4 ply Cotton in White (A)
- Small amount of Rowan Lurex Shimmer in Mauve (C)
- Small amount of Rowan Kidsilk Haze in Mauve (D)
- Scraps of Yellow, Black and Pink sport weight wool
- Washable toy stuffing
- Pair each of 2 (2¾ mm) and 3 (3 mm) knitting needles
- Size C (2.50 mm) crochet hook

ABBREVIATIONS
See page 14.

GAUGE
4 ply cotton gauge for body:
32 sts and 42 rows to 4 in. (10 cm) measured over stockinette stitch using 2 (2¾ mm) needles.
4 ply cotton gauge for dress:
29 sts and 39 rows to 4 in. (10 cm) measured over stockinette stitch using 3 (3 mm) needles.
Kidsilk Haze gauge for sleeves:
25 sts and 34 rows to 4 in. (10 cm) measured over stockinette stitch using 3 (3 mm) needles.

PRINCESS

1ST LEG
With 2 (2¾ mm) needles and MC, cast on 18 sts.
Work 12 rows in st st.
Shape heel: K 9 sts, turn, sl 1, p7, turn, sl 1, k6, turn. Continue until p 3, then turn. Sl 1, k2, turn, sl 1, p to end.
Work even in st st for 44 rows. Bind off.

2ND LEG
Work as for first leg, working heel on last 9 sts on needle instead of first 9 sts.

BODY
With 2 (2¾ mm) needles and A, cast on 44 sts.
Work in st st as follows:
Work 2 rows A, 2 rows MC for 10 rows.
Change to MC.
Work 24 rows, ending with a WS row.
Shape armholes: K10 sts, bind off 2, k to last 12 sts, bind off 2, k to end.
Work on these last 10 sts in st st.
Work 1 row.
Next row: RS facing: Dec 1, k to end. (9 sts.)
Work even in st st for 5 rows.
Next row: Bind off 5 sts, k4. Break yarn.

FRONT
Rejoin yarn to center 20 sts with WS facing.
Work 1 row.
Dec 1 st at each end of next row. (18 sts.)
Work even for 5 rows.
Next row: Bind off 5 sts, k to last 5 sts, bind off rem 5 sts. Break yarn.

LEFT BACK
Rejoin yarn to rem 10 sts with WS facing and work 1 row.
Dec 1 st at end of next row.
Work even for 5 rows.
Next row: K4, bind off 5 sts. Break yarn.

With RS facing k across all neck sts, inc 4 sts evenly. (20 sts.)
Work 3 rows st st.

HEAD
Knit into front and back of every st. (40 sts.)
Cast on 1 st at beg of next 4 rows. (44 sts.)
Work 13 rows even.
Next row: *K2tog, k9; rep from * to end. (40 sts.)
Next row: Purl.
Next row: *K2tog, k8; rep from * to end. (36 sts.)
Dec as estalished until 20 sts rem.
Break off yarn and thread through rem sts.

ARMS (make 2)
With 2 (2¾ mm) needles and MC, cast on 4 sts.
Work 6 rows in st st.
Break yarn and set these thumb sts to one side.
With 2 (2¾ mm) needles and MC, cast on 12 sts.
Work 8 rows in st st. Break yarn.
Next row: K4 thumb sts, then k12 from "hand".
Work 5 rows st st.
7th row: K2tog, k14. (15 sts.)
Work 32 rows even.
Dec 1 st at beg of next row and at same edge on foll 3 rows. (11 sts.)
Work 4 rows even.
Dec 1 st at beg of next row and at same edge on foll 3 rows. (7 sts.)
Bind off.

FINISHING
Sew leg seams and stuff. Sew arm seams and stuff.
Attach legs to cast-on edge of body, leaving a small gap for crotch. Sew up back seam.
Set arms into armholes. Stuff body and head.
Using Black, embroider French knots for eyes and satin stitch for nose. Embroider mouth using stem stitch and Pink.
Cut lengths of yellow yarn approx 13 in. (33 cm) long. Using backstitch, stitch to center of head to form hair. Plait hair at side of face and secure. With C, make tightly twisted strand of yarn to hold in place.

SOCKS
1ST SOCK
With 2 (2¾ mm) needles and A, cast on 18 sts.
Work 12 rows in st st.
Shape heel
K9 sts, turn, sl 1, p7, turn, sl 1, k6, turn.
Continue until p3, then turn. Sl 1, k2, turn, sl 1, p to end.
Work even in st st for 10 rows. Bind off.
2ND SOCK
Work as for first sock, working heel on last 9 sts on needle instead of first 9 sts. Sew seam.

EDGING ON SOCKS
With size C (2.50 mm) crochet hook and A, work a row of dc along top edge of socks, then work as follows:
1 dc into the first st, *ch3 , skip one st, 1 dc into next st, rep from * to end.
Fasten off.

SHOES (make 2)
With 2 (2¾ mm) needles and B, cast on 9 sts.
Work in st st, inc 1 st at beg of every row until there are 15 sts.
K2tog at beg of every row until 9 sts rem.
Cast on 6 sts, k to end. (15 sts.) Inc 1 st at beg of next row, then every other row until there are 18 sts.
Next row: [RS] Bind off 10 sts, k to end. (8 sts.)
Work 9 rows. Cast on 10 sts at beg of next row. (18 sts.)
Dec 1 st at beg of next row, then every other row until 15 sts rem.
Bind off.
Sew heel and sole seams.
Make ties:
Cut two 7-in. (18-cm) lengths of C, thread through top of shoes and tie in bow to form laces.

DRESS
FRONT
With 3 (3 mm) needles and B, cast on 72 sts.
Work in st st until 40 rows have been worked.
Next row: [RS] k2, [k2tog] to last 2 sts, k2. (38 sts.)
Next row: P2, [p2tog] to last 2 sts, p2. (21 sts.)
Work 4 rows even.

Shape armholes
Bind off 2 sts at beg of next 2 rows. (17 sts.)
Dec 1 st at each end of next row. (15 sts.)
Work even in st st for 11 rows.
Shape front neck
RS facing: K4, leave rem sts on a spare needle. Work
another 3 rows even on these 4 sts. Bind off.
Rejoin yarn to rem sts with RS facing, cast off center
7 sts, k to end. Work another 3 rows even on these 4
sts. Bind off.

BACK
With 3 (3 mm) needles and B, cast on 72 sts.
Work in st st until 40 rows have been worked.
Next row: [RS] k2, [k2tog], to last 2 sts, k2. (38 sts.)
Next row: P2, [p2tog] to last 2 sts, p2. (21 sts.)
Work 4 rows even.
Shape armholes
Bind off 2 sts at beg of next 2 rows. (17 sts.)
Dec 1 st at each end of next row. (15 sts.)
Work 1 row.
Divide for back opening
K 7, leave rem sts on a spare needle. Work even for
another 10 rows.
WS facing: Bind off 2 sts, p to end. (5 sts.) Dec 1 st at
neck edge on next row. (4 sts.)
Work 1 row even. Bind off rem sts.
Return to rem sts left on spare needle, k2tog, k to
end. (7 sts.) Work 9 rows.
Bind off 2 sts at beg of next row. (5 sts.)
Dec 1 st at neck edge on next row. Work even for
2 rows. Bind off rem sts.

SLEEVES
With 3 (3 mm) needles and D, cast on 25 sts, work in
st st for 16 rows. Bind off.
With 2 (2¾ mm) needles and C, cast on 3 sts, work in
g st until work measures 1¾ in. (4.5 cm) (width of
arm). Bind off.

PETALS [make 10]
With 3 (3 mm) needles and D, cast on 2 sts. Inc 1 st at
each end of foll 3 rows. (8 sts.) Work even for 9 rows.

Dec 1 st at each end EOR twice. Work 1 row.
Bind off rem 4 sts.

FINISHING
Join shoulder seams. Set in sleeves, gathering
sleeves at top. Gather lower edge and sew g st band
to cast-on edge of sleeves.
Sew side and sleeve seams.

BODICE BAND
With 2 (2¾ mm) needles and C, cast on 3 sts, work in
g st until work measures 10 in. (26 cm).
Bind off.

HEM EDGING
With a size C (2.50 mm) crochet hook and C, work a
row of dc along cast-on edge of dress, then work as
follows:
1 dc into the first st, *ch3, skip 1 st, 1 dc into next st,
rep from * to end.

NECK EDGING
Work as for hem edging.
Cut 10-in. (25-cm) lengths of C and attach center of
each length to neck edge at top of back opening. Tie
in bow to fasten neck.
Sew petals in place on Back and Front, gathering
petals.
Sew bodice band in place neatly starting and
finishing at center back, just covering top of petals.
Tie bow.

With C, embroider "stars" around lower edge of
"skirt" part of dress (see page 12).

CROWN
With 2 (2¾ mm) needles and C, cast on 2 sts.
1st row: Knit.
2nd row: Knit.
3rd row: Cast on 2 sts, k to end.
4th row: Knit.
5th row: Bind off 2 sts, k to end.
Rep from 2nd to 5th row 15 more times, or until long
enough to fit round head.
Bind off.
Join cast-on and cast-off seams.

Monkey

This playful knitted toy is great for your own little monkeys and will appeal to anyone with a sense of fun. Rowan Kid Classic is a lovely soft yarn, making this a cuddly toy as well.

MEASUREMENTS
15 in. (38 cm) tall

MATERIALS
• 1 x 50 g ball of Rowan Kid Classic in Medium Brown (MC)
• 1 x 50 g ball of Rowan Kid Classic in Light Brown (A)
• Small amount Black for embroidery
• Pair 5 (3¾ mm) knitting needles
• Washable toy stuffing

ABBREVIATIONS
See page 14.

GAUGE
20 sts and 27 rows to 4 in. (10 cm) measured over stockinette stitch using 5 (3¾ mm) needles.

LEGS
With 5 (3¾ mm) needles and MC, cast on 14 sts.
Beg with a k row, work 44 rows in st st.
Bind off.

ARMS
With 5 (3¾ mm) needles and MC, cast on 14 sts.
Beg with a k row, work 44 rows in st st.
Bind off.

BODY
With 5 (3¾ mm) needles and MC, cast on 17 sts for neck edge.
P 1 row.
Next row: K1, [m1, k1] 7 times, k2, [m1, k1] 7 times. (31 sts.)
Work 5 rows.
Next row: [K5, m1] 3 times, k1, [m1, k5] 3 times. (37 sts.)

Work 3 rows.
Next row: [K6, m1] 3 times, k1, [m1, k6] 3 times. (43 sts.)
Work 27 rows.
Next row: [K8, skp] twice, k3, [k2tog, k8] twice. (39 sts.)
P 1 row.
Next row: [K7, skp] twice, k3, [k2tog, k7] twice. (35 sts.)
P 1 row.
Bind off.

HEAD
With 5 (3¾ mm) needles and MC, cast on 13 sts.
P 1 row.
Next row: K1, [m1, k1] to end. (25 sts.)
P 1 row.
Next row: K1, [m1, k2] to end. (37 sts.)
St st 3 rows.
Next row: [K9, m1] twice, k1, [m1, k9] twice. (41 sts.)
P 1 row.
Next row: K20, m1, k1, m1, k20. (43 sts.)
St st 15 rows.
Next row: [K8, skp] twice, k3, [k2tog, k8] twice. (39 sts.)
P 1 row.
Next row: [K7, skp] twice, k3, [k2tog, k7] twice. (35 sts.)
P 1 row.
Next row: [K6, skp] twice, k3, [k2tog, k6] twice. (31 sts.)
St st 3 rows.
Next row: K1, [k2tog, k1] to end. (21 sts.)
P 1 row.
Next row: K1, [k2tog] to end. (11 sts.)
Next row: P1, [p2tog] to end. (6 sts.)
Break off yarn, thread through rem sts, pull up tightly and fasten off securely.

MUZZLE

With 5 (3¾ mm) needles and A, cast on 32 sts.
Beg with a k row work 6 rows st st.
Next row: K2tog, [k1, k2tog] to end. (21 sts.)
P 1 row.
Next row: K1, [k2tog] to end. (11 sts.)
Break yarn, thread through rem sts, pull up tightly and fasten off securely.

EYE PIECE

With 5 (3¾ mm) needles and A, cast on 19 sts.
Beg with a k row work 6 rows st st.
Next row: K1, [k2tog] to end. (10 sts.)
Break yarn, thread through rem sts, pull up tightly and fasten off securely.

FEET

With 5 (3¾ mm) needles and A, cast on 8 sts.
Beg with a p row, work 3 rows st st.
Inc 1 st at each end of next row, then EOR twice, then on foll 4th row. (16 sts.)
St st 3 rows.
Next row: K2tog, k3, turn, leave rem sts.
P 1 row.
Next row: K2tog, k2.
Next row: P2tog, p1.
K2tog and fasten off. Rejoin yarn to inside of rem sts, k to last 2 sts, k2tog. (10 sts.)

P 1 row.
Next row: K2tog, k to last 2 sts, k2tog.
Bind off rem 8 sts.
Make another piece exactly the same, then make another two pieces, reversing shapings, by reading p for k and k for p.

HANDS

Work as given for feet.

TAIL

With 5 (3¾ mm) needles and MC, cast on 9 sts.
Beg with a K row, work in st st for 48 rows.
Next row: K2tog, k5, k2tog.
St st 3 rows.
Next row: K2tog, k3, k2tog.
P 1 row.
Next row: K2tog, k1, k2tog.
K3tog and fasten off.
Break yarn, thread through rem sts, pull up tightly and fasten off securely.

EARS

With 5 (3¾ mm) needles and MC, cast on 11 sts.
Beg with a K row, work in st st for 6 rows.
Dec 1 st at each end of next row, then EOR once. (7 sts.)
Work 1 row.
Bind off.
Make another piece using MC, then make another 2 pieces using A.

FINISHING

Join outside edges of feet to make a pair. Join cast-on edge to cast-on edge of legs. Join leg seam, stuff and join top seam.
Fold sides of cast-off edge of body to center and sew it together, join back seam. Stuff firmly. Gather neck edge, pull up and secure. Join outside edges of hands to make a pair. Join cast-on edge to cast-on edge of arms. Join arm seam, stuff and join top seam. Attach arms and legs to body.
Join head seam, leaving an opening, stuff and join opening. Attach to body. Join eye piece seam, sew to head. Join muzzle seam, sew to head, stuffing lightly.
Sew pairs of ears together, leaving cast-on edges open, then sew ears to sides of head.
Embroider eyes and nostrils in satin stitch and mouth in stem stitch using Black.

Pig

This adorable piglet is a perfect size for a little friend to take on a trip to the farm. Knitted in soft baby pink wool, this faithful piglet can easily be tucked under a child's arm.

MEASUREMENTS
Approximately 6¼ in. (16 cm) tall

MATERIALS
- 2 x 50 g balls of Jaeger Baby Merino DK in Pale Pink
- Scraps of Jaeger Baby Merino DK in Black
- Pair 3 (3¼ mm) knitting needles
- Washable toy stuffing

ABBREVIATIONS
See page 14.

GAUGE
24 sts and 32 rows to 4 in. (10 cm) measured over stockinette stitch using 3 (3¼ mm) needles.

UPPER BODY
With 3 (3¼ mm) needles and Pale Pink, cast on 76 sts.
K 1 row.
Shape back legs
Cont in st st.
Cast on 3 sts at beg of next 4 rows and 6 sts at beg of foll 2 rows. (100 sts.)
St st 12 rows.
Bind off 6 sts at beg of next 2 rows and 3 sts at beg of foll 4 rows. (76 sts.)
St st 35 rows.
Shape front legs
Cast on 12 sts at beg of next 2 rows. (100 sts.)
St st 10 rows.
Bind off 12 sts at beg of next 2 rows. (76 sts.)
St st 10 rows.

Shape head
Next row: K16, [k2tog tbl, k9] twice, [k9, k2tog] twice, k16.
St st 3 rows.
Next row: K16, [k2tog tbl, k8] twice, [k8, k2tog] twice, k16.
St st 3 rows.
Place marker at each end of last row.
Next row: K16, [k2tog tbl, k7] twice, [k7, k2tog] twice, k16. (64 sts.)
P 1 row.
Cont in this way, dec 4 sts as established EOR 5 times. (44 sts.)
St st 9 rows.
Next row: K6, [k twice in next st, k5] 6 times, k2. (50 sts.)
P 1 row.
Bind off.

UNDERBODY

With 3 (3¼ mm) needles and Pale Pink, cast on 3 sts.
K 1 row.
Cont in st st, inc 1 st at each end of next 3 rows, then EOR 4 times. (17 sts.)
St st 6 rows.
Dec 1 st at each end of next row, then EOR twice. (11 sts.)
St st 5 rows.
Mark each end of last row.

Shape back legs

Cast on 3 sts at beg of next 6 rows and 6 sts at beg of foll 2 rows. (41 sts.)
Next row: K15, k2tog tbl, k7, k2tog, k15.
St st 2 rows.
Next row: P14, p2tog, p7, p2tog tbl, p14.
St st 2 rows.
Next row: K13, k2tog tbl, k7, k2tog, k13.
St st 2 rows.
Next row: P12, p2tog, p7, p2tog tbl, p12.

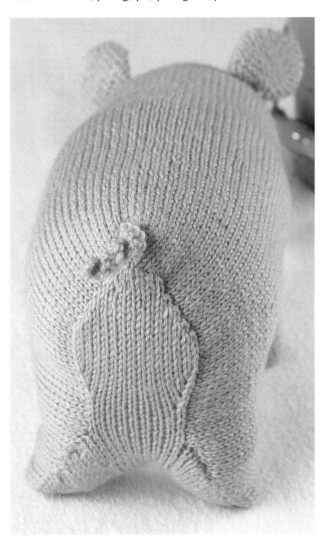

St st 2 rows.
Bind off 3 sts at beg of next 2 rows.
Next row: Bind off 3 sts, k until there are 5 sts on right needle, k2tog tbl, k7, k2tog, k5.
Bind off 3 sts at beg of next 3 rows. (13 sts.)
St st 34 rows.

Shape front legs

Cast on 12 sts at beg of next 2 rows. (37 sts.)
St st 10 rows.
Bind off 12 sts at beg of next 2 rows. (13 sts.)
St st 8 rows.
Dec 1 st at each end of the next row, then EOR 4 times.
P 1 row.
Bind off.

SNOUT

With 3 (3¼ mm) needles and Pale Pink, cast on 3 sts.
K 1 row.
Cont in g st, inc 1 st at each end of the next 3 rows, then EOR 3 times. K 7 rows.
Dec 1 st at each end of next row, then EOR twice, then on 3 foll rows.
K 1 row.
Bind off.

EARS (make 2)

With 3 (3¼ mm) needles and Pale Pink, cast on 17 sts.
K 6 rows.
Dec 1 st at each end of the next row, then every 4th row twice, then EOR 4 times.
K 1 row.
K3tog and fasten off.

TAIL

With 3 (3¼ mm) needles and Pale Pink, cast on 20 sts loosely. Bind off tightly.

FINISHING

Join seam from bind-off edge to marker. Sew in snout. Leaving a gap, join upperbody to underbody, matching legs and continue back seam to center of cast-on sts. Stuff and close opening.
Fold sides of ear to center at cast-on edge and secure. Sew on ears and tail.
Embroider eyes and nostrils in satin stitch using Black.
Embroider mouth in stem stitch using Black.

Zebra

Go wild with this crazy striped zebra and imagine being in the hot, sunny grasslands of Africa. This simple, yet effective toy is knitted in bold black and white double knitting yarn.

MEASUREMENTS
Approximately 12½ in. (32 cm) high

MATERIALS
- 1 x 50 g ball of Jaeger Matchmaker Merino DK in Black
- 1 x 50 g ball of Jaeger Matchmaker Merino DK in White
- Scrap of brown yarn for facial features
- Pair of 3 (3¼ mm) knitting needles
- Washable toy stuffing

ABBREVIATIONS
See page 14.

GAUGE
24 sts and 32 rows to 4 in. (10 cm) measured over stockinette stitch using 3 (3¼ mm) needles.

LEGS
With 3 (3¼ mm) needles and Black, cast on 20 sts.
Beg with a K row, cont in st st, working 2 rows Black, then stripes of 4 rows White and 4 rows Black.
Work 6 rows.
Dec 1 st at end of next row.
Work 9 rows.
Dec 1 st at beg of next row.
Work 21 rows.
Dec 1 st at each end of next 3 rows.
Bind off rem 12 sts.

ARMS
With 3 (3¼ mm) needles and White, cast on 7 sts.
Beg with a K row, cont in st st, working 2 rows White, then stripes of 4 rows Black, and 4 rows White.
Work 1 row.
Inc 1 st at each end of next 4 rows. (15 sts.)
Work 7 rows.

Dec 1 st at end of next row.
Work 9 rows.
Dec 1 st at beg of next row.
Work 11 rows.
Shape for hand
Cont in Black only.
Work 1 row.
Inc 1 st at each end of next 2 rows. (17 sts.)
Work 5 rows.
Next row: K1, skp, k3, k2tog, k1, skp, k3, k2tog, k1. (13 sts.)
Next row: P.
Next row: K1, skp, k1, k2tog, k1, skp, k1, k2tog, k1. (9 sts.)
Next row: P.
Next row: K1, sl 1, k2tog, psso, k1, sl 1, k2tog, psso, k1.
Break yarn, thread through rem 5 sts and fasten off.

BACK BODY
With 3 (3¼ mm) needles and Black, cast on 6 sts.
Beg with a K row, cont in st st, working 2 rows Black, then stripes of 4 rows White and 4 rows Black.
Work 2 rows.
Next row: K1, * m1, k1; rep from * to end. (11 sts.)
Work 3 rows.
Next row: K1, [m1, k2] 5 times. (16 sts.)
Work 3 rows.
Next row: K2, [m1, k3] 4 times, m1, k2. (21 sts.)
Work 3 rows.
Next row: K3, [m1, k4] 4 times, m1, k2. (26 sts.)
Work 23 rows.
Next row: K1, [k2tog, k3] 5 times. (21 sts.)
Work 3 rows.
Next row: K1, [k2tog, k2] 5 times. (16 sts.)
Work 3 rows.
Next row: K1, [k2tog, k1] 5 times. (11 sts.)
Work 3 rows.
Bind off rem 11 sts.

FRONT BODY

With 3 (3¼ mm) needles and Black, cast on 6 sts.
Beg with a K row, cont in st st, working 2 rows Black,
then stripes of 4 rows White and 4 rows Black.
Work 2 rows.
Next row: K1, [m1, k1] 5 times. (11 sts.)
Work 3 rows.
Next row: K1, [m1, k2] 5 times. (16 sts.)
Work 3 rows.
Next row: K2, [m1, k2] 7 times. (23 sts.)
Work 3 rows.
Next row: K2, [m1, k3] 7 times. (30 sts.)
Work 23 rows.
Next row: K2, [k2tog, k6] 3 times, k2tog, k2. (26 sts.)
Work 3 rows.
Next row: K2, k2tog, k5, k2tog, k4, k2tog, k5, k2tog,
k2. (22 sts.)
Work 3 rows.
Next row: K2, [k2tog, k1] 6 times, k2. (16 sts.)
Work 3 rows.
Bind off rem 16 sts.

HEAD

With 3 (3¼ mm) needles and White, cast on 7 sts.
P 1 row.
Next row: K1, [m1, k1] to end.
Rep the last 2 rows once more. (25 sts.)
P 1 row.
Next row: K3, [m1, k2] to end. (36 sts.)
P 1 row.
Next row: K3, [m1, k3] to end. (47 sts.)
P 1 row.
Next row: K3, [m1, k4] to end. (58 sts.)
Work 3 rows in st st.
Next row: K48, turn.
Next row: P38, turn.
Next row: K34, turn.
Next row: P30, turn.
Next row: K26, turn.
Next row: P22, turn.
Next row: K18, turn.
Next row: P14, turn.
Next row: K10, turn.
Next row: P6, turn.

Next row: K to end.
Work 7 rows in st st.
Next row: K10, k2tog, k6, skp, k18, k2tog, k6, skp, k10. (54 sts.)
Next row: P to end.
Next row: K9, k2tog, k6, skp, k16, k2tog, k6, skp, k9.
Next row: P to end.
Next row: K8, k2tog, k6, skp, k14, k2tog, k6, skp, k8.
Next row: P to end.

Next row: K7, k2tog, k6, skp, k12, k2tog, k6, skp, k7.
Next row: P to end.
Next row: K6, k2tog, k6, skp, k10, k2tog, k6, skp, k6.
Next row: P to end.
Next row: K5, k2tog, k6, skp, k8, k2tog, k6, skp, k5. (34 sts.)
Change to Black.
Next row: P to end.
Next row: K4, k2tog, k6, skp, k6, k2tog, k6, skp, k4.
Work 3 rows.
Next row: K3, k2tog, k6, skp, k4, k2tog, k6, skp, k3.
Work 3 rows.
Next row: K2, k2tog, k6, skp, k2, k2tog, k6, skp, k2. (22 sts.)
Work 3 rows.
Next row: K4, skp, k2tog, k6, skp, k2tog, k4.
Work 1 row.
Next row: K3, skp, k2tog, k4, skp, k2tog, k3.
Work 1 row.
Bind off rem 14 sts.

EARS (make 2 pairs)
With 3 (3¼ mm) needles and White, cast on 12 sts.
Work 8 rows in st st.
Change to Black.
Dec 1 st at each end of the next 5 rows.
Work 2 tog and fasten off.

FINISHING
Join leg and arm seams, stuff. Join side and cast-on edges of body, stuff. Join seam of head.
With seam to center of bind-off edge, join "nose" seam, stuff. Join head to body.
Attach arms and legs to body. Sew pairs of ears, stuff lightly, sew to top of head along line formed by turning rows.
With Black work a row of loops between ears.
Embroider French knots for eyes in Black and French knots for nostrils in Brown.
Using Brown, embroider mouth in stem stitch.
For tail, make a twisted cord in Black, 3 in. (8 cm) long. Knot one end and trim to form a short tassel. Attach the other end to back of body.

Dog draft cheater

This cuddly dog, knitted in a soft aran yarn, is almost too good to be used as a draft cheater and would probably be more comfortable lying on a sofa.

SKILL LEVEL 3

MEASUREMENTS
35½ in. (90 cm) long

MATERIALS
- 4 x 100 g balls of Jaeger Shetland in Brown (Bark Tweed)
- 1 x 100 g ball of Jaeger Shetland in each of Cream (Linen Tweed) and Black
- Pair of 3 (3¼ mm) knitting needles
- Washable toy stuffing

ABBREVIATIONS
See page 14.

GAUGE
26 stitches and 32 rows to 4 in. (10 cm) measured over stockinette stitch using 3 (3¼ mm) needles.

BODY TOP
Left back leg: With 3 (3¼ mm) needles and Brown, cast on 26 sts. Beg with a k row, st st 32 rows. Break off yarn and leave these sts on a st holder.
Right back leg: With 3 (3¼ mm) needles and Brown, cast on 26 sts. Beg with a k row, st st 32 rows.
Joining row: K to end, then k across sts of left back leg. (52 sts.) St st another 27 rows.
Using separate small balls of yarn for each colored area and twisting yarns together on WS at join, reading k rows from right to left and p rows from left to right, work 40 rows of chart. Cont in st st in Brown only, work another 140 rows.
Shape front legs: Next row: K24, bind off next 4 sts, k to end.

Left front leg: Work in st st on last set of 24 sts for another 47 rows. Bind off.
Right front leg: With wrong side facing, rejoin yarn to rem 24 sts and work in st st for another 47 rows. Bind off.

BODY UNDERSIDE
Using Brown throughout, work as for Body Top.

BACK LEG SOLES (make 2)
With 3 (3¼ mm) needles and Brown, cast on 8 sts. K 1 row. Cont in st st, inc 1 st at each end of next 3 rows. Work 1 row. Inc 1 st at each end of next row and foll 4th row. (18 sts.) St st 5 rows. Dec 1 st at each end of next row and foll 4th row. Work 1 row. Dec 1 st at each end of next 3 rows. (8 sts.) Bind off.

☐ Brown
☒ Cream

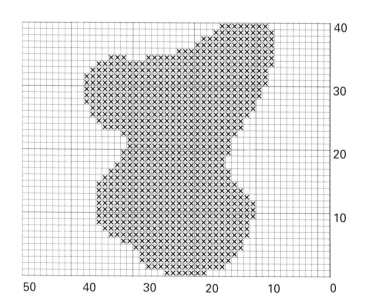

FRONT LEG SOLES (make 2)

With 3 (3¼ mm) needles and Brown, cast on 6 sts. K 1 row. Cont in st st, inc 1 st at each end of next 2 rows. Work 1 row. Inc 1 st at each end of next row and foll 3rd row. (14 sts.)

St st 3 rows. Dec 1 st at each end of next row and foll 3rd row. Work 1 row. Dec 1 st at each end of next 2 rows. (6 sts.)

Bind off.

RIGHT SIDE HEAD

With 3 (3¼ mm) needles and Brown, cast on 13 sts for neck edge. K 1 row. Mark end of last row.

Shape neck and back edge: 1st row: P to last st, inc.

2nd row: Inc, k to last st, inc.

3rd row: P to last st, inc.

4th row: Inc, k to end. Rep these 4 rows, twice more, then work 1st and 2nd row again. (31 sts.)

Mark beg of last row. St st 3 rows. Inc 1 st at end of next row. (32 sts.) Work 1 row.

Shape chin: Cast on 3 sts at beg of next row, then EOR 7 times. (56 sts.)

Mark beg of last row. St st 3 rows.

Shape top: Bind off 6 sts at beg of next row, then EOR once, then 12 sts at beg of EPO twice. (20 sts.)

Bind off rem sts.

LEFT SIDE HEAD

Work as given for Right Side Head, reversing shapings by reading p for k and k for p.

TOP GUSSET

With 3 (3¼ mm) needles and Brown, cast on 12 sts.
Beg with a k row, work in st st, inc 1 st at each end of 3rd row, foll 4th row and foll 6th row. (18 sts.)
St st 4 rows.
Using separate small balls of yarn for each colored area and twisting yarns together on wrong side at join, work as follows:

1st row: P15 Brown, 3 Cream.
2nd row: With Cream, inc, k4, with Brown, k12, inc.
3rd row: P12 Brown, 8 Cream.
4th row: K9 Cream, 11 Brown.
5th row: P10 Brown, 10 Cream.
6th row: K11 Cream, 9 Brown.
7th row: With Brown, inc, p8, with Cream, p10, inc.
8th row: K13 Cream, 9 Brown.
9th row: With Brown, inc, p8, with Cream, p12, inc.
10th row: K14 Cream, 10 Brown.
11th row: With Brown, inc, p9, with Cream, p13, inc.
12th row: K15 Cream, 11 Brown.
13th row: With Brown, inc, p10, with Cream, p14, inc.
14th row: With Cream, inc, k15, with Brown, k11, inc.
15th row: With Brown, inc, p12, with Cream, p16, inc.
16th row: With Cream, inc, k17, with Brown, k13, inc.

17th row: P15 Brown, 19 Cream.
18th row: K18 Cream, 16 Brown.
19th row: P16 Brown, 18 Cream.
20th row: With Cream, inc, k16, with Brown, k16, inc.
21st row: P18 Brown, 18 Cream.
22nd row: K17 Cream, 19 Brown.
23rd row: P20 Brown, 16 Cream.
24th row: With Cream, inc, k14, with Brown, k20, inc. (38 sts.)
25th row: P24 Brown, 14 Cream.
26th row: K12 Cream, 26 Brown.
27th row: P28 Brown, 10 Cream.
28th row: K6 Cream, 32 Brown.
Cont in Brown only, st st 15 rows. Mark each end of last row. Dec 1 st at each end of next 2 rows. (34 sts.)
Next row: Dec, k10, [skp] twice, k2, [k2tog] twice, k10, dec. Dec 1 st at each end of next row. (26 sts.)

Next row: Dec, k6, [skp] twice, k2, [k2tog] twice, k6, dec. Dec 1 st at each end of next row. (18 sts.)
Next row: Dec, k2, [skp] twice, k2, [k2tog] twice, k2, dec. Dec 1 st at each end of next row. (10 sts.)
Bind off.

UNDERCHIN GUSSET

With 3 (3¼ mm) needles and Brown, cast on 16 sts. Cont in st st, inc 1 st at each end of 7th row, then every 6th row 4 times. (26 sts.) St st 13 rows. Dec 1 st at each end of next 8 rows. (10 sts.) Bind off.

EARS (make 4)

With 3 (3¼ mm) needles and Brown, cast on 12 sts. Cont in st st, inc 1 st at each end of 5th row, then every 6th row 5 times. (24 sts.) St st 21 rows. Dec 1 st at each end of next 4 rows. (16 sts.) Bind off.

NOSE

With 3 (3¼ mm) needles and Black, cast on 8 sts. K 1 row. Cont in st st, inc 1 st at each end of next 4 rows. (16 sts.) St st 11 rows. Dec 1 st at each end of next 4 rows. (8 sts.) Bind off.

EYES (make 2)

With 3 (3¼ mm) needles and Black, cast on 3 sts. K 1 row. Cont in st st, inc 1 st at each end of next 2 rows. (7 sts.) St st 4 rows. Dec 1 st at each end of next 2 rows. (3 sts.) Bind off.

LEFT SIDE TAIL

With 3 (3¼ mm) needles and Brown, cast on 19 sts. Beg with a k row, st st 2 rows.
1st row: K to last 2 sts, dec. P 1 row.
3rd row: Inc, k to last 2 sts, dec. P 1 row. Rep these 4 rows, 3 times. (15 sts.)
Next row: K to last 2 sts, dec. P 1 row. Rep last 2 rows, 4 more times. (10 sts.) Bind off.

RIGHT SIDE TAIL

Work as given for Left Side Tail, reversing shapings by reading p for k and k for p.

TAIL TOP

With 3 (3¼ mm) needles and Black, cast on 10 sts. K 1 row, p 1 row.
Next row: Inc in each st to end. (20 sts.) P 1 row.
Next row: [K1, inc] to end. (30 sts.) St st 3 rows.
Next row: [K2, inc] to end. (40 sts.) St st 5 rows.

Next row: [K2, dec] to end. (30 sts.) St st 3 rows.
Next row: [K1, dec] to end. (20 sts.) P 1 row.
Next row: [Dec] to end. (10 sts.) Break off yarn, leaving a long end. Thread end through sts, pull up and secure.

FINISHING

Join body pieces together, leaving cast-on and bind-off edges of legs open and small opening at side. Sew in soles. Stuff body firmly and close opening. Join head sides together along back edge. Place top of this seam against center of cast-on edge of top gusset and, matching markers on gusset to markers at top of chin shaping on sides, sew in top gusset. Line up cast-on edge of underchin gusset with markers at beginning of chin shaping on sides and sew in underchin gusset.

Stuff head firmly, position on body near front legs and stitch in place.

Join paired ear pieces together, position on head and sew in place. Run a gathering thread around nose piece and pull up lightly, stuff the nose, pull the thread tightly and secure. Position nose on head and stitch in place.

Run a gathering thread around each eye piece, pull up tightly and secure. Position on head and stitch in place.

Join tail pieces together, leaving cast-on and bind-off edge free. Join top tail along row ends, stuff firmly and sew to bind-off edge of tail, then stuff tail. Sew cast-on edge of tail to body.

Small teddy bear

Every bear needs a friend and this little teddy is well worth your affection. Because of his size, he can be carried everywhere in a pocket or bag.

MEASUREMENTS
Teddy: approximately 8 in. (20 cm) high
Scarf: 15 x 1 in. (38 x 2.5 cm)

MATERIALS
- 1 x 50 g ball of Rowan Kid Classic in Light Natural (MC)
- 1 x 50 g ball of Rowan Kid Classic in Caramel (A)
- Scraps of Patons Diploma Gold DK in Blue, Yellow and Red
- Pair of 3 (3¼ mm) knitting needles
- Size D (3.25 mm) crochet hook
- Washable toy stuffing
- Brown embroidery thread for facial features

ABBREVIATIONS
See page 14.

GAUGE
Teddy: 24 sts and 32 rows to 4 in. (10 cm) measured over stockinette stitch using 3 (3¼ mm) needles.

BEAR
LEGS (make 2)
With 3 (3¼ mm) needles and MC, cast on 26 sts.
Beg with a K row, work 5 rows st st.
Next row: P13, turn.
Work on this set of sts only.
Dec 1 st at beg of next row, then EOR once, then at end of next row. (10 sts.)
Break off yarn and rejoin at inside edge to second set of sts, p to end.
Dec 1 st at end of next row, then EOR once, then at beg of next row. (10 sts.)
K 1 row across all sts. (20 sts.)
Work 18 rows.

Next row: P10, turn and work on this set of sts only.
Dec 1 st at each end of next 2 rows. (6 sts.)
Bind off.
Rejoin yarn to rem sts and complete to match first side.

SOLES (make 2)
With 3 (3¼ mm) needles and A, cast on 3 sts.
Beg with a k row cont in st st.
K 1 row.
Inc 1 st at each end of the next 2 rows, then EOR once. (9 sts.)
Work 6 rows even.
Dec 1 st at each end of the next row, then EOR once, then on foll row. (3 sts.)
Work 1 row.
Bind off.

ARMS (make 2)
* With 3 (3¼ mm) needles and MC, cast on 4 sts.
Beg with a k row work 2 rows in st st.
Inc 1 st at each end of next row, then EOR once.
Work 1 row *.
Break off yarn.
Rep from * to *.
K 1 row across all sts. (16 sts.)
Inc 1 st at each end of 2nd row and foll 4th row. (20 sts.)
Work 15 rows even.
Next row: K10, turn.
Work on this set of sts only.
Dec 1 st at each end of next 2 rows. (6 sts.)
Work 1 row.
Bind off.
Rejoin yarn to rem sts and complete as for first side.

BODY (make 2)

* With 3 (3¼ mm) needles and MC, cast on 3 sts.
Beg with a k row cont in st st.
Work 1 row.
Inc 1 st at each end of the next 2 rows, then EOR twice. (11 sts.) *.
Break off yarn.
Rep from * to *.
P 1 row across both sets of sts. (22 sts.)
Work 12 rows even.
Dec 1 st at each end of next row, then every 3rd row twice, then EOR once. (14 sts.)
Work 1 row.
Bind off.

BACK HEAD

With 3 (3¼ mm) needles and MC, cast on 3 sts.
K 1 row.
Cont in st st, inc 1 st at each end of next 2 rows, then at end of foll 3 rows. (10 sts.)
Work 1 row.
Inc 1 st at beg of next row. (11 sts.)
K 1 row.
Break off yarn.

Using MC cast on 3 sts.
K 1 row.
Cont in st st, inc 1 st at each end of next 2 rows, then at beg of foll 3 rows. (10 sts.)
Work 1 row.
Inc 1 st at end of next row. (11 sts.)
K 1 row.
P 1 row across all sts. (22 sts.)
Work 6 rows even.
Next row: K11, turn.
Work on this set of sts only.
Dec 1 st at each end of next row.
Work 1 row.
Dec 1 st at end of next 3 rows.
Mark end of last row.
Dec 1 st at each end of next row. (4 sts.)
Work 1 row.
Bind off.
Rejoin at inside edge to rem sts, k to end.
Dec 1 st at each end of next row.
Work 1 row.
Dec 1 st at beg of next 3 rows.
Mark beg of last row.
Dec 1 st at each end of next row. (4 sts.)
Work 1 row.
Bind off.

HEAD GUSSET

With 3 (3¼ mm) needles and MC, cast on 11 sts.
Work 4 rows st st.
Dec 1 st at each end of next row, then EOR once, then on foll row.
Work 2 rows.
Dec 1 st at each end of next row.
Work 1 row.
Work 3 tog and fasten off.

RIGHT SIDE OF HEAD

With 3 (3¼ mm) needles and MC, cast on 6 sts.
Beg with a k row, cont in st st.
Work 1 row.
Inc 1 st at beg of next row.
Inc 1 st at each end of next row and beg of foll 4 rows, then at end of next row.
Inc 1 st at beg of next row. (15 sts.)
Work 5 rows even.
Mark end of last row.
Bind off 2 sts at beg of next row.
Dec 1 st at end of next row and at beg of foll row. (11 sts.)
* Dec 1 st at each end of next row, then at beg of foll row *.
Rep from * to *. (5 sts.)
Work 1 row.
Mark beg of last row. Bind off.

LEFT SIDE OF HEAD

Work as given for Right side of head, reversing shapings.

EARS (make 2 in MC and 2 in A)

With 3 (3¼ mm) needles, cast on 6 sts.
Work 3 rows st st.
Dec 1 st at each end of next 2 rows.
Bind off.

FINISHING

Note: Purl side of knitting is used as right side.
Join instep, top and inner back leg seams leaving an opening.
Sew in soles. Stuff and close opening. Join arm seams, leaving an opening. Stuff and close opening.
Join center seam on each body piece, join body pieces together, leaving bind-off edge open.
Stuff and gather open edge, pull up and secure.
Join sides of head from cast-on edge to first marker.
Sew in head gusset, placing point at center front seam and cast-on edge in line with second markers

on sides of head. Join center seams of back head, then sew to front head, matching markers and leaving cast-on edge open.
Stuff and gather open edge, pull up and secure. Sew head to body.
Attach yarn about ½ in. (1 cm) below top of one arm, thread through body at shoulder position, then attach other arm, pull yarn tightly and thread through body again in same place, then attach to first arm and fasten off.
Attach legs in same way. Join paired ear pieces together and sew them in place.
Using brown embroidery thread, embroider eyes and nose in satin stitch and mouth in straight stitch.

SCARF

With 3 (3¼ mm) needles and Blue, cast on 7 sts and work in g st as follows:
2 rows Blue, 2 rows Yellow, 2 rows Red.
These 6 rows form rep of patt, cont in stripe patt until scarf meas 15 in. (38 cm), ending with 2 rows Blue.
Bind off.
Make fringe of 5 tassels at each end of scarf, using Blue (see page 13).

Large teddy bear

Cute and cuddly pretty much sums up this guy: all he wants is care and attention, but careful – you may fall in love with him before the children can get him!

SKILL LEVEL 3

MEASUREMENTS
Approximately 14 in. (36 cm) high

MATERIALS
• 2 x 50 g balls of Rowan Kid Classic in Light Natural (MC)
• 1 x 50 g ball of Rowan Kid Classic in Caramel (A)
• 2 x 50 g balls of Patons Diploma Gold DK in Red
• Pair each of 3 (3¼ mm) and 6 (4 mm) knitting needles
• Washable toy stuffing
• Brown embroidery thread for facial features

ABBREVIATIONS
See page 14.

GAUGE
Teddy: 24 sts and 32 rows to 4 in. (10 cm) measured over stockinette stitch using 3 (3¼ mm) needles.
Sweater: 22 sts and 30 rows to 4 in. (10 cm) measured over stockinette stitch using 6 (4 mm) needles.

BEAR
LEGS (make 2)
With 3 (3¼ mm) needles and MC, cast on 50 sts.
Beg with a K row, work 10 rows st st.
Next row: K25, turn.
Work on this set of sts only.
Dec 1 st at beg of next row, then EOR 3 times, then at end of next row and beg of foll row. (19 sts.)
Work 1 row.
Break off yarn and rejoin at inside edge to second set of sts, k to end.
Dec 1 st at end of next row, then EOR 3 times, then at beg of next row and end of foll row. (19 sts.)

Work 1 row.
P 1 row across all sts. (38 sts.)
Work 27 rows.
Next row: P19, turn and work on this set of sts only.
Dec 1 st at each end of next row, then EOR twice, then on 2 foll rows. (9 sts.)
Work 1 row.
Bind off.
Rejoin yarn to rem sts and complete to match first side.

SOLES (make 2)
With 3 (3¼ mm) needles and A, cast on 5 sts.
Beg with a k row cont in st st.
K 1 row.
Inc 1 st at each end of the next 3 rows, then EOR once. (13 sts.)
Work 11 rows even.
Dec 1 st at each end of the next row, then foll 4th row, then EOR once, then at each end of the next 2 rows. (3 sts.)
Bind off.

Work 20 rows even.
Next row: P19, turn.
Work on this set of sts only.
Dec 1 st at each end of next row, then EOR twice, then on 2 foll rows. (9 sts.)
Work 1 row.
Bind off.
Rejoin yarn to rem sts and complete as for first side.

BODY (make 2)

* With 3 (3¼ mm) needles and MC, cast on 7 sts.
Beg with a k row cont in st st.
Work 1 row.
Inc 1 st at each end of the next 2 rows then EOR 5 times. (21 sts.)
Work 1 row *.
Break off yarn.
Rep from * to *.
K 1 row across both sets of sts. (42 sts.)
Work 25 rows even.
Dec 1 st at each end of next row, then every 4th row twice, then EOR 3 times, then on every row until 20 sts rem.
Bind off.

BACK HEAD

With 3 (3¼ mm) needles and MC, cast on 7 sts.
K 1 row.
Cont in st st, inc 1 st at each end of next 2 rows, then at end of foll 5 rows. (16 sts.)
Work 1 row.
Inc 1 st at beg of next 2 rows. (18 sts.)
Break off yarn.
Using MC, cast on 7 sts.
K 1 row.
Cont in st st, inc one st at each end of next 2 rows, then at beg of foll 5 rows.
Work 1 row.
Inc 1 st at end of next 2 rows. (18 sts.)
P 1 row across all sts. (36 sts.)
Work 22 rows even.
Next row: K2tog, k16, turn.
Work on this set of sts only.
Dec 1 st at each end of every 3rd row twice, then EOR once. (11 sts.)
Mark beg of last row.
Dec 1 st at end of next row, each end of foll row and at end of next row. (7 sts.)
Bind off.
Rejoin at inside edge to rem sts, k to last 2 sts, k2tog.
Dec 1 st at each end of every 3rd row twice, then EOR

ARMS (make 2)

* With 3 (3¼ mm) needles and MC, cast on 8 sts.
Beg with a k row work 2 rows in st st.
Inc 1 st at each end of next row, then EOR once.
Work 1 row *.
Inc 1 st at beg of next row.
Work 1 row.
Inc 1 st at each end of foll row. (15 sts.)
Work 1 row.
Break off yarn.
Rep from * to *.
Inc 1 st at end of next row.
Work 1 row.
Inc 1 st at each end of foll row. (15 sts.)
Work 1 row.
K 1 row across all sts. (30 sts.)
Inc 1 st at each end of 2nd row, then every 6th row 3 times.
(38 sts.)

once. Mark end of last row.
Dec 1 st at beg of next row, each end of foll row and at beg of next row. (7 sts.)
Bind off.

HEAD GUSSET

With 3 (3¼ mm) needles and MC, cast on 20 sts.
Work 10 rows in st st.
Dec 1 st at each end of next row, then every 4th row 3 times, then EOR 3 times. (6 sts.)
Work 3 rows.
Dec 1 st at each end of next 2 rows.
Work 2 tog and fasten off.

RIGHT SIDE OF HEAD

With 3 (3¼ mm) needles and MC, cast on 10 sts.
Beg with a k row, cont in st st.
Work 1 row.
Inc 1 st at beg of next row.
Inc 1 st at each end of next row and beg of foll 6 rows, then at end of next row. (20 sts.)
Inc 1 st at each end of next row. (22 sts.)
Inc 1 st at end of next row and at same edge on foll 3 rows. (26 sts.)
Work 11 rows even.

Mark end of last row.
Bind off 2 sts at beg of next row. (24 sts.)
Dec 1 st at end of next row and at same edge on foll 6 rows. (17 sts.)
Dec 1 st at each end of next row, then at end of foll row.
Dec 1 st at each end EOR once. (12 sts.)
Work 1 row.
Dec 1 st at end of next 3 rows. (9 sts.)
Work 1 row.
Mark end of last row.
Bind off.

LEFT SIDE OF HEAD

Work as given for Right side of head, reversing shapings.

EARS (make 2 in MC and 2 in A)

With 3 (3¼ mm) needles cast on 13 sts.
Work 5 rows in st st.
Dec 1 st at each end of next 5 rows. (3 sts.)
Bind off.

FINISHING

Note: Purl side of knitting is used as right side.

Join instep, top and inner back leg seams leaving an opening.

Sew in soles. Stuff and close opening. Join arm seams, leaving an opening.

Stuff and close opening. Join center seam on each body piece, join body pieces together, leaving bind-off edge open.

Stuff and gather open edge, pull up and secure. Join sides of head from cast-on edge to first marker.

Sew in head gusset, placing point at center front seam and cast-on edge in line with second markers on sides of head.

Join center seams of back head, then sew to front head, matching markers and leaving cast-on edge open.

Stuff and gather open edge, pull up and secure. Sew head to body.

Attach yarn about ½ in. (1 cm) below top of one arm, thread through body at shoulder position, then attach other arm, pull yarn tightly and thread through body again in same place, then attach to first arm and fasten off.

Attach legs in same way. Join paired ear pieces together and sew them in place.

Using brown embroidery thread, embroider eyes and nose in satin stitch and mouth in straight stitch.

SWEATER

BACK

With 3 (3¼ mm) needles and Red, cast on 42 sts.

Beg with a k row, work 4 rows in st st.

Change to 6 (4 mm) needles.

Beg with a k row, work in st st throughout, until Back meas 6 in. (16 cm) from beg, ending with a WS row.

Shape shoulders

Bind off 10 sts at beg of next 2 rows.

Leave rem 22 sts on a holder.

FRONT

Work as for Back until work meas 5 in. (13 cm) from beg, ending with a WS row.

Shape neck

Next row: K15, turn.

Work on this set of sts only.

Dec 1 st at neck edge on every row until 10 sts rem.

Work even until Front matches Back to shoulder shaping, ending at armhole edge.

Shape shoulder

Bind off 10 sts at beg of next row.

With RS facing, rejoin yarn to rem sts, sl center 12 sts on to a holder, k to end.

Complete to match first side, reversing shapings, work an extra row before start of shoulder shaping.

SLEEVES

With 3 (3¼ mm) needles and Red, cast on 28 sts.

Beg with a k row, work 4 rows in st st.

Change to 6 (4 mm) needles.

Beg with a k row, work in st st throughout, shaping sides by inc 1 st at each end of 3rd row, then every 4th row until there are 34 sts.

Work even until Sleeve meas 4½ in. (11 cm), ending after a WS row.

NECKBAND

Join right shoulder seam.

With 3 (3¼ mm) needles and RS facing, pick up 9 sts down left front neck, k center 12 sts, pick up 9 sts up right front neck, k 22 back neck sts. (52 sts.)

Beg with a p row, work 9 rows in rev st st. Bind off.

FINISHING

Join left shoulder seam, reversing seam on st st roll.

Sew on sleeves, reversing seam on st st roll.

Join side and sleeve seams, reversing seam on st st roll.

Girl rag doll

This bright and cheerful girl rag doll has all the appeal of a
traditional old-fashioned doll and yet is still a great toy for any
little girl. You can knit a whole wardrobe for her by altering
the colors and textures of the sweater, skirt and shoes.

SKILL LEVEL 3

MEASUREMENTS
Approximately 15 in. (36 cm) high

MATERIALS
• 1 x 50 g ball of Rowan 4 ply Cotton in Light Pink
• 1 x 50 g ball of Rowan 4 ply Soft in Red
• 1 x 50 g ball of Rowan 4 ply Soft in Pink
• 1 x 25 g ball of Rowan Kidsilk Haze in Fuchsia
• Scraps of 4 ply in Yellow, Black and Pink
• Pair each of 2 (2¾ mm) and 3 (3¼ mm) knitting
  needles
• Washable toy stuffing
• Shirring elastic

ABBREVIATIONS
See page 14.

GAUGE
4 ply Cotton
32 sts and 42 rows to 4 in. (10 cm) measured over
stockinette stitch using 2 (2¾ mm) needles.
Kidsilk Haze
25 sts and 34 rows to 4 in. (10 cm) measured over
stockinette stitch using 3 (3¼ mm) needles.

DOLL
BACK
With 2 (2¾ mm) needles and Light Pink, cast on 43
sts.
Beg with a k row, work 44 rows in st st.
Mark each end of last row with a colored thread.
Work another 51 rows.
Next row: P20, bind off next 3 sts, p to end.
Cont in stripes of 2 rows Red and 2 rows Pink.
Cont on last set of sts for first leg.

Work 52 rows in st st.
Mark each end of last row. **
Work 6 rows.
Cont in Red only.
Shape Heel
Next row: K11, skp, k1, turn.
Next row: P4, p2tog, p1, turn.
Next row: K5, skp, k1, turn.
Next row: P6, p2tog, p1, turn.
Cont in this way, dec 1 st as established on every row
until 12 sts rem, ending with a p row.
Break yarn and leave these sts on a holder.
Now cont in stripes of 2 rows Pink and 2 rows Red.
With RS facing and beg at marker, pick up and k 8 sts
from side of heel, k12 sts from holder, pick up and
k 8 sts from other side of heel to marker. (28 sts.)

Cont in st st, dec 1 st at each end of every 4th row 4
times. (20 sts.)
Work 7 rows.
Shape Toes
*** **Next row:** K1, skp, k to last 3 sts, k2tog, k1.
P 1 row.
Rep last 2 rows once more. (16 sts.)
K 1 row.
Next 2 rows: P 11, turn, k to end.
Next 2 rows: P6, turn, k to end. ***
Break yarn and leave these sts on a spare needle.
With RS facing, rejoin yarn to rem sts for second leg
and work as given for first leg, reversing shaping.

FRONT
Work as given for Back to **.
Work another 24 rows in st st.
Shape Toes
Work as given for Back from *** to ***.
With RS of back and front together and taking 1 st
from each needle and working them tog, bind off toe
sts.
With right side facing, rejoin yarn to rem sts for
second leg and complete as given for first leg,
reversing toe shaping.

ARMS (make 2)
With 2 (2¾ mm) needles and Light Pink, cast on 30
sts.
Beg with a k row work 46 rows in st st.
Shape thumb
Next row: K15, m1, k15.
P 1 row.
Next row: K15, m1, k1, m1, k15.
P 1 row.
Next row: K15, m1, k3, m1, k15.
P 1 row.
Next row: K15, m1, k5, m1, k15.
P 1 row.
Next row: K22, turn and cast on 1 st.
Next row: P8, turn and cast on 1 st.
Work 4 rows on these 9 sts.
Next row: K1, [k2tog] 4 times.
Break yarn, thread end through rem sts, pull up,
secure, then sew thumb seam.
With RS facing, rejoin yarn at base of thumb, pick up
and k2 sts from base of thumb, k to end. (32 sts.)
Work 9 rows.
Shape fingers
Next 2 rows: Work to last 4 sts, turn.
Next 2 rows: Work to last 8 sts, turn.

Next 2 rows: Work to last 12 sts, turn.
Next row: K4.
With RS together, fold arm in half, taking 1 st from
each needle and working them together, bind off.

FINISHING
Join back and front together, leaving cast-on edge
free. Stuff firmly.
Wind a length of yarn twice around neck edge, pull
up tightly and secure.
Stuff head, gather cast-on edge, pull up and secure,
join gathers to form a seam across top of head. Work
a few lines of stitching in feet to form toes.
Sew arm seams, leaving end open, stuff firmly and
close opening. Work a few lines of stitching in hands
to form fingers. Sew to side seams of body.

FACIAL FEATURES
Work in satin stitch for nose in Light Pink.
Work French knots using 6 wraps for eyes in Black.
Work stem stitch for mouth in Pink.

HAIR
Cut yellow yarn into 17-in. (43-cm) lengths. Backstitch center of lengths into position at the center part
on doll's head from just above neck at back to
forehead. Using Pink, make 2 twisted cords and
thread through side of head. Tie hair into position
and trim hair.

SKIRT

Using 2 (2¾mm) needles and Pink, cast on 60 sts.
Work 6 rows single rib.
Change to 3 (3¼mm) needles.
Cont in st st.
Work 2 rows.
Inc row: K8, m1, k to last 8 sts, m1, k8.
Work 3 rows.
Rep the last 4 rows 5 more times. (72 sts.)
K 4 rows.
Bind off.

FINISHING

Join side seams. Thread shirring elastic through waist to fit doll.

SWEATER

BACK

With 2 (2¾mm) needles and Pink, cast on 56 sts.
Beg with a k row, work 6 rows in st st.
Change to 3 (3¼mm) needles and Fuchsia.
Work 34 rows in st st.

Shape neck

Next row: K16, turn, and work on these sts for first side of neck.
Dec 1 st at neck edge on next 3 rows. (13 sts.)
Bind off.
With RS of work facing slip center 24 sts onto a holder.
Rejoin yarn to next st, k to end.

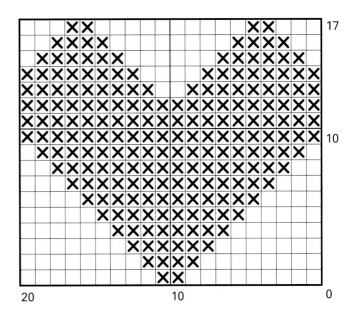

☐ Fuchsia
☒ Pink

Complete to match first side of neck shaping.

FRONT

Work as given for back until 12 rows have been worked in Fuchsia.

Place motif

Next row: K18, work across row 1 of Chart, k18.
Using the intarsia method, cont to end of Chart.
Work another 3 rows.

Shape neck

Next row: K18, turn, and work on these sts for first side of neck.

Dec 1 st at neck edge on next 5 rows. (13 sts.)

Bind off.

With right side of work facing slip center 20 sts on a holder.

Rejoin yarn to next st, k to end.

Complete to match first side of neck shaping.

Neckband

Join right shoulder seam.

With right side facing, using 2 (2¾mm) needles and Pink, pick up and k6 sts down left side of front neck, k across 20 sts at center front, pick up and k 6 sts up right side of front neck, 4 sts down right side of back neck, k across 24 sts at center back neck, pick up and k 4 sts up left side of back neck. (64 sts.)

Beg with a p row,'work 5 rows in st st.

Bind off.

SLEEVES

With 2 (2¾mm) needles and Pink cast on 38 sts.

Work 6 rows in st st.

Change to 3 (3¼mm) needles and Fuchsia.

Inc and work into st st 1 st at each end of the 3rd and 3 foll 4th rows. (46 sts.)

Work even to 4½ in. (11 cm), ending with a p row.

Bind off.

Join left shoulder and neckband seam. Sew on sleeves. Sew side and sleeve seams.

GIRL'S SHOES

With 3 (3¼ mm) needles and Red, cast on 48 sts.

K1 row.

1st row: K1, yo, k22, yo, k2, yo, k22, yo, k1.

2nd and 4th rows: K to end, working k1 tbl into yo of previous row.

3rd row: K2, yo, k23, yo, k2, yo, k23, yo, k2.

5th row: K3, yo, k24, yo, k2, yo, k24, yo, k3. (60 sts.)

6th row: K to end, working k1 tbl into yo of previous row.

K10 rows.

Shape top

Next row: K27, k2tog, k2, skp, k27.

K1 row.

Next row: K26, k2tog, k2, skp, k26.

K1 row.

Next row: K25, k2tog, k2, skp, k25.

K1 row.

Bind off rem 54 sts.

Join back and sole seam. Make 2 twisted cords and thread through bind-off edge to tie at center front.

Boy rag doll

Why limit yourself to just a girl rag doll when you can knit a boy rag doll too? You can make a whole wardrobe of clothes and let your child play dress up with her or his doll.

SKILL LEVEL 3

MEASUREMENTS
Approximately 14 in. (36 cm) high

MATERIALS
- 2 x 50 g balls of Rowan 4 ply Cotton in Pale Pink
- 1 x 50 g ball of Rowan 4 ply Soft in each of Gray and Turquoise
- 1 x 25 g ball of Rowan Kidsilk Haze in Light Gray
- Scraps of DK Brown for hair, sport weight Black for eyes and Pink for mouth and nose
- Pair each of 2 (2¾ mm) and 3 (3 mm) knitting needles
- Washable toy stuffing
- Shirring elastic

ABBREVIATIONS
See page 14.

GAUGE
4 ply Cotton
32 sts and 42 rows to 4 in. (10 cm) measured over stockinette stitch using 2 (2¾ mm) needles.
Kidsilk Haze
25 sts and 34 rows to 4 in. (10 cm) measured over stockinette stitch using 3 (3¼ mm) needles.

DOLL
BACK
With 2 (2¾ mm) needles and Pale Pink, cast on 43 sts.
Beg with a k row, work 44 rows in st st.
Mark each end of last row with a colored thread.
Cont in st st for another 51 rows.
Next row: P20, bind off next 3 sts, p to end.
Cont on last set of sts for first leg.
Work 52 rows in st st.
Mark each end of last row. **
Work 6 rows.
Shape Heel
Next row: K11, skp, k1, turn.
Next row: P4, p2tog, p1, turn.
Next row: K5, skp, k1, turn.
Next row: P6, p2tog, p1, turn.
Cont in this way, dec 1 st as established on every row until 12 sts rem, ending with a p row.
Break yarn and leave these sts on a holder.
With RS facing and beg at marker, pick up and k 8 sts from side of heel, k12 sts from holder, pick up and k 8 sts from other side of heel to marker. (28 sts.)
Cont in st st, dec 1 st at each end of 4 foll 4th rows. (20 sts.)
Work 7 rows.
Shape Toes
*** **Next row:** K1, skp, k to last 3 sts, k2tog, k1.
P 1 row.
Rep last 2 rows once more. (16 sts.)
K 1 row.
Next 2 rows: P 11, turn, k to end.
Next 2 rows: P6, turn, k to end. ***
Break yarn and leave these sts on a spare needle.
With RS facing, rejoin yarn to rem sts for second leg and work as given for first leg, reversing shaping.

FRONT

Work as given for Back to **.

Work another 24 rows in st st.

Shape Toes

Work as given for Back from *** to ***.

With RS of back and front together and taking 1 st from each needle and working them tog, bind off toe sts.

With RS facing, rejoin yarn to rem sts for second leg and complete as given for first leg, reversing toe shaping.

ARMS (make 2)

With 2 (2¾ mm) needles and Pale Pink, cast on 30 sts. Beg with a k row work 46 rows in st st.

Shape thumb

Next row: K15, m1, k15.

P 1 row.

Next row: K15, m1, k1, m1, k15.

P 1 row.

Next row: K15, m1, k3, m1, k15.

P 1 row.

Next row: K15, m1, k5, m1, k15.

P 1 row.

Next row: K22, turn and cast on 1 st.

Next row: P8, turn and cast on 1 st.

Work 4 rows on these 9 sts.

Next row: K1, [k2tog] 4 times.

Break off yarn, thread end through rem sts, pull up, secure, then sew thumb seam.

With RS facing, rejoin yarn at base of thumb, pick up and k 2 sts from base of thumb, k to end. (32 sts.) Work 9 rows.

Shape fingers

Next 2 rows: Work to last 4 sts, turn.

Next 2 rows: Work to last 8 sts, turn.

Next 2 rows: Work to last 12 sts, turn.

Next row: K4.

With RS together, fold arm in half, taking 1 st from each needle and working them together, bind off.

FINISHING

Join back and front together, leaving cast-on edge free. Stuff firmly. Wind a length of yarn twice round neck edge, pull up tightly and secure. Stuff head, gather cast-on edge, pull up and secure, join gathers to form a seam across top of head. Work a few lines of stitching in feet to form toes. Sew arm seams, leaving end open, stuff firmly and close opening. Work a few lines of stitching in hands to form fingers. Sew to side seams of body.

FACIAL FEATURES

Work in satin stitch for nose in Pale Pink.

Work French knots using 6 wraps for eyes in Black.

Work stem stitch for mouth in pink.

HAIR

Make fringe by sewing loops of brown yarn at top of head to front of forehead. Cut loops to form fringe. Cut brown yarn into 8-in. (20-cm) lengths. Back stitch the center of lengths into position of the center part on doll's head from just above neck at back to forehead. Trim hair.

PANTS

Using 2 (2¾ mm) needles and Turquoise, cast on 60 sts.

Work 6 rows single rib.

Change to 3 (3¼ mm) needles.

Cont in st st until leg measures 3¼ in. (8½ cm) from cast-on edge.

Shape crotch

Bind off 3 sts at beg of next 2 rows. (54 sts.)

Inc 1 st at each end of the next row, then every 6th row until there are 60 sts.

Work 2 rows.

K4 rows.

Bind off.

FINISHING

Sew inner leg seams. Sew front and back seam. Thread shirring elastic through waist to fit doll.

SWEATER

BACK

With 2 (2¾ mm) needles and Turquoise, cast on 57 sts.

Beg with a k row, work 6 rows in st st.

Change to 3 (3¼ mm) needles and Light Gray.

Work 34 rows in st st.

Shape neck

Next row: K16, turn, and work on these sts for first side of neck.

Dec 1 st at neck edge on next 3 rows. (13 sts.)

Bind off.

With RS of work facing slip center 25 sts on a holder. Rejoin yarn to next st, k to end.

Complete to match first side of neck shaping.

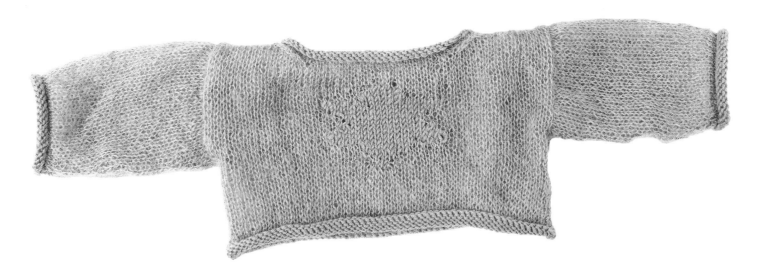

FRONT

Work as given for back until 12 rows have been worked in light gray.

Place motif

Next row: K19, work across row 1 of Chart, k19. Using the intarsia method, cont to end of Chart. Work another 3 rows.

Shape neck

Next row: K18, turn, and work on these sts for first side of neck.

Dec 1 st at neck edge on next 5 rows. (13 sts.)
Bind off.

With RS of work facing slip center 21 sts on a holder. Rejoin yarn to next st, k to end.

Complete to match first side of neck shaping.

Neckband

Join right shoulder seam.

With RS facing, using 2 (2¾ mm) needles and Turquoise, pick up and k6 sts down left side of front neck, k across 21 sts at center front, pick up and k 6 sts up right side of front neck, 4 sts down right side of back neck, k across 25 sts at center back neck, pick up and k 4 sts up left side of back neck.
(66 sts.)

Beg with a p row, work 5 rows in st st.
Bind off.

SLEEVES

With 2 (2¾ mm) needles and Turquoise, cast on 38 sts.

Work 6 rows in st st.

Change to 3 (3¼ mm) needles and Light Gray.

Inc and work in st st 1 st at each end of the 3rd row,

then every 4th row 3 times. (46 sts.)

Work even to 4½ in. (11 cm), ending with a p row.
Bind off.

FINISHING

Join left shoulder and neckband seam. Sew on sleeves. Join side and sleeve seams.

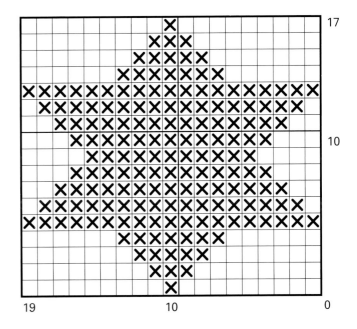

Light Gray

☒ Turquoise

SOCKS

With 3 (3¼ mm) needles and Turquoise, cast on 36 sts.

Rib row: * K1, p1; rep from * to end.

Rib another 9 rows.

Change to 3 (3 mm) needles.

Work 10 rows rib, dec 4 sts on last row. (32 sts.)

Change to 3 (3¼ mm) needles.

Beg with a k row, cont in st st.

Work 5 rows.

Shape heel

Next row: P9 sts only, turn.

Work 9 rows in st st on these 9 sts only.

Dec row: P3, p2tog, p1, turn.

Next row: Sl 1, k4.

Dec row: P4, p2tog, p1, turn.

Next row: Sl 1, k5.

Dec row: P5, p2tog.

Break yarn and leave rem 6 sts on a holder.

With WS facing, slip center 14 sts on to a holder, rejoin yarn to rem 9 sts, p to end.

Work 8 rows in st st on these 9 sts.

Dec row: K3, k2tog tbl, k1, turn.

Next row: Sl 1, p4.

Dec row: K4, k2tog tbl, k1, turn.

Next row: Sl 1, p5.

Dec row: K4, k2tog tbl, k1, turn.

Next row: Sl 1, p5.

Shape instep

Next row: K6, pick up and k 8 sts evenly along inside edge of heel, k 14 sts from holder, pick up and k 8 sts along inside edge of heel and k 6 sts from holder. (42 sts.)

P 1 row.

Dec row: K12, k2tog, k14, k2tog tbl, k12.

P 1 row.

Dec row: K11, k2tog, k14, k2tog tbl, k11.

P 1 row.

Dec row: K10, k2tog, k14, k2tog tbl, k10.

P 1 row.

Dec row: K9, k2tog, k14, k2tog tbl, k9. (34 sts.)

Work 17 rows even.

Shape toes

Dec row: K6, k2tog, k2, skp, k10, k2tog, k2, skp, k6.

P 1 row.

Dec row: K5, k2tog, k2, skp, k8, k2tog, k2, skp, k5.

P 1 row.

Dec row: K4, k2tog, k2, skp, k6, k2tog, k2, skp, k4.

P 1 row.

Dec row: K3, k2tog, k2, skp, k4, k2tog, k2, skp, k3.

P 1 row. Bind off rem sts.

Sew back of foot seam.

SHOES

With 3 (3¼ mm) needles and Gray, cast on 48 sts.

K 1 row.

1st row: K1, yo, k22, yo, k2, yo, k22, yo, k1.

2nd and 4th rows: K to end, working k1 tbl into yo of previous row.

3rd row: K2, yo, k23, yo, k2, yo, k23, yo, k2.

5th row: K3, yo, k24, yo, k2, yo, k24, yo, k3. (60 sts.)

6th row: K to end, working k1 tbl into yo of previous row.

K 10 rows.

Shape top

Next row: K27, k2tog, k2, skp, k27.

K 1 row.

Next row: K26, k2tog, k2, skp, k26.

K 1 row.

Next row: K25, k2tog, k2, skp, k25.

K 1 row.

Next row: K24, k2tog, k2, skp, k24.

K 1 row.

Next row: K23, k2tog, k2, skp, k23.

K 1 row.

Next row: K22, k2tog, k2, skp, k22.

K 1 row.

Bind off rem 48 sts.

Join back and sole seam. Make two 12-in. (30-cm) long twisted cords and thread through bind-off edge to tie at center front.

Panda

The endangered Giant Panda is one of the most popular animals in the world. This gorgeous knitted toy will appeal to children of all ages.

SKILL LEVEL 3

MEASUREMENTS
13 in. (33 cm) high

MATERIALS
- 3 x 50 g balls of Jaeger Matchmaker Merino DK in Black
- 2 x 50 g balls of Jaeger Matchmaker Merino DK in White
- Pair of 7 (4½ mm) knitting needles
- Washable toy stuffing

Use two strands of yarn together throughout.

ABBREVIATIONS
See page 14.

GAUGE
19 stitches and 27 rows to 4 in. (10 cm) measured over stockinette stitch using 7 (4½ mm) needles.

BODY FRONT (make 1)
Crotch gusset: With 7 (4½ mm) needles and White, cast on 3 sts. Mark center st. Beg with a k row, cont in st st, work 1 row. Inc 1 st at each end of next 8 rows, then EOR twice. (23 sts.) P 1 row. Mark each end of last row.
Shape legholes: Bind off 2 sts at beg of next 2 rows. Dec 1 st at each end of next row, then EOR once, then every 3rd row twice. (11 sts.) St st 5 rows. Inc 1 st at each end of next 10 rows, thus completing leghole shaping. (31 sts.)
St st 10 rows.
Using separate small balls of yarn for each colored area and twisting yarns together on wrong side at join, cont as follows:
1st row: K2 Black, 27 White, 2 Black.
2nd row: P5 Black, 21 White, 5 Black.

3rd row: K8 Black, 15 White, 8 Black.
4th row: P11 Black, 9 White, 11 Black.
5th row: K13 Black, 5 White, 13 Black.
Cont in Black only, p 1 row.
Shape armholes: Bind off 2 sts at beg of next 2 rows. Dec 1 st at each end of next row, then EOR 3 times. (19 sts.)
Shape neck: Next row: P5, bind off next 9 sts, p to end. **Next row:** K2tog, k1, k2tog, turn.
Next row: P2tog, p1. K2tog and fasten off.
Rejoin yarn at inside edge to rem 5 sts, k2tog, k1, k2tog.
Next row: P1, p2tog. K2tog and fasten off.

BODY BACK (make 1)
First side: With 7 (4½ mm) needles and White, cast on 3 sts. Beg with a k row, cont in st st, work 1 row. Mark end of last row. P 1 row. Cast on 3 sts at beg of next row, then EOR twice. (12 sts.) P 1 row. Leave these sts.
Second side: With 7 (4½ mm) needles and White, cast on 3 sts. Beg with a k row, cont in st st, work 1 row. Mark beg of last row. Cast on 3 sts at beg of next row, then EOR 3 times. (15 sts.) Mark 2nd sts from beg of last row.
Joining row: K15 sts from second side then 12 sts from first side. (27 sts.)
St st 9 rows. Inc 1 st at each end of next 8 rows, thus completing leghole shaping. (43 sts.) St st 10 rows. Cont as follows:
1st row: K2 Black, 39 White, 2 Black.
2nd row: P4 Black, 35 White, 4 Black.
3rd row: K6 Black, 31 White, 6 Black.
4th row: P7 Black, 29 White, 7 Black.
5th row: K8 Black, 27 White, 8 Black.
6th row: P9 Black, 25 White, 9 Black.
Shape armholes: 7th row: With Black, bind off 2 sts, k 7 sts more, 23 White, 10 Black.
8th row: With Black, bind off 2 sts, p 8 sts more, 21 White, 9 Black.

9th row: With Black, k2tog, k8, 19 White, with Black, k8, k2tog.

10th row: P11 Black, 15 White, 11 Black.

11th row: With Black, k2tog, k11, 11 White, with Black, k11, k2tog.

12th row: P14 Black, 7 White, 14 Black.

Cont in Black only, dec 1 st at each end of next row, then EOR 3 times. (27 sts.)

Shape neck: Next row: P8, bind off next 11 sts, p to end.

Next row: K2tog, k6, turn. Bind off 3 sts at beg of next row. (4 sts.) Bind off rem sts.

Rejoin yarn at inside edge to rem 8 sts, bind off 3 sts, k2 more sts, k2tog. (4 sts.) P 1 row. Bind off rem sts.

RIGHT LEG (make 1)

With 7 (4½ mm) needles and Black, cast on 41 sts. Beginning with a k row, st st 6 rows.

Shape instep: Next row: K24, [k2tog, k1] twice, k2tog, k9.

Next row: P8, bind off next 7sts, p to end.

Next row: Inc, k21, k2tog, k6, inc. (32 sts.)

Inc 1 st at each end of every 4th row twice. (36 sts.) St st 3 rows.

Shape top: Bind off 4 sts at beg of next 2 rows.

Dec 1 st at each end of next row then EOR twice, then on next 3 rows. Bind off 3 sts at beg of next 2 rows. (10 sts.) Bind off.

LEFT LEG (make 1)

Work as given for right leg, reversing shapings, by reading p for k and k for p.

SOLES (make 2)

With 7 (4½ mm) needles and Black, cast on 5 sts. K 1 row. Cont in st st, inc 1 st at each end of next 2 rows, then EOR twice. (13 sts.) St st 7 rows. Dec 1 st at each end of next row, then EOR twice. Dec 1 st at each end of next row. (5 sts.) Bind off.

RIGHT ARM (make 1)

With 7 (4½ mm) needles and Black, cast on 13 sts. Beg with a k row, st st 2 rows.

1st inc row: Inc, k4, inc, k1, inc, k4, inc. (17 sts.) P 1 row.

2nd inc row: K2, inc, [k3, inc] 3 times, k2. (21 sts.) P 1 row.

3rd inc row: K2, inc, [k4, inc] 3 times, k3. (25 sts.) P 1 row.

4th inc row: K3, inc, [k5, inc] 3 times, k3. (29 sts.) St st 7 rows. **

Shape elbow: 1st row: K26, yfwd, sl 1, yb, turn.

2nd row: Sl 1, p11, yb, sl 1, yfwd, turn.

3rd row: Sl 1, k8, yfwd, sl 1, yb, turn.

4th row: Sl 1, p5, yb, sl 1, yfwd, turn.

5th row: Sl 1, k7, yfwd, sl 1, yb, turn.

6th row: Sl 1, p9, yb, sl 1, yfwd, turn.

7th row: Sl 1, k11, yfwd, sl 1, yb, turn.

8th row: Sl 1, p13, yb, sl 1, yfwd, turn.

9th row: Sl 1, k15.

St st 5 rows across all sts.

Shape top: Bind off 2 sts at beginning of next 2 rows. Dec 1 st at each end of next row , then EOR 4 times. (15 sts.) P 1 row.

Next row: Bind off 4 sts, k to last 2 sts, dec. Rep last 2 rows, once more. (5 sts.) Bind off.

LEFT ARM (make 1)

Work as for right arm to **.

Shape elbow: 1st row: K14, yfwd, sl 1, yb, turn.

2nd row: Sl 1, p11, yb, sl 1, yfwd, turn.

3rd row: Sl 1, k8, yfwd, sl 1, yb, turn.

4th row: Sl 1, p5, yb, sl 1, yfwd, turn.

5th row: Sl 1, k7, yfwd, sl 1, yb, turn.

6th row: Sl 1, p9, yb, sl 1, yfwd, turn.

7th row: Sl 1, k11, yfwd, sl 1, yb, turn.

8th row: Sl 1, p13, yb, sl 1, yfwd, turn.

9th row: Sl 1, k27.

St st 5 rows across all sts.

Shape top: Bind off 2 sts at beginning of next 2 rows. Dec 1 st at each end of next row, then EOR 4 times. (15 sts.) P 1 row. Dec 1 st at beg of next row. Bind off 4 sts at beg of next row. Rep last 2 rows, once more. (5 sts.) Bind off.

HEAD

With 7 (4½ mm) needles and White, cast on 14 sts. Beg with a k row, st st 2 rows.

Shape back head: Cast on 4 sts at beg of next 8 rows. (46 sts.) K 1 row.

1st row: P43, yb, sl 1, yfwd, turn.

2nd row: Sl 1, k40, yfwd, sl 1, yb, turn.

3rd row: Sl 1, p38, yb, sl 1, yfwd, turn.

4th row: Sl 1, k36, yfwd, sl 1, yb, turn.

5th row: Sl 1, p34, yb, sl 1, yfwd, turn.

6th row: Sl 1, k32, yfwd, sl 1, yb, turn.

7th row: Sl 1, p30, yb, sl 1, yfwd, turn.

8th row: Sl 1, k28, yfwd, sl 1, yb, turn.

9th row: Sl 1, p25, yb, sl 1, yfwd, turn.

10th row: Sl 1, k22, yfwd, sl 1, yb, turn.

11th row: Sl 1, p19, yb, sl 1, yfwd, turn.

12th row: Sl 1, k16, yfwd, sl 1, yb, turn.

13th row: Sl 1, p13, yb, sl 1, yfwd, turn.
14th row: Sl 1, k10, yfwd, sl 1, yb, turn.
15th row: Sl 1, p7, yb, sl 1, yfwd, turn.
16th row: Sl 1, k4, yfwd, sl 1, yb, turn.
Next row: Sl 1, p to end.
Inc row: Cast on 3 sts, k these 3 sts, k5, inc, [k4, inc] 7 times, k5, turn and cast on 3 sts. (60 sts.) P 1 row.
Shape top head: 1st row: Cast on 4 sts, k these 4 sts, k35, yfwd, sl 1, yb, turn.
2nd row: Sl 1, p10, yb, sl 1, yfwd, turn.
3rd row: Sl 1, k14, yfwd, sl 1, yb, turn.
4th row: Sl 1, p18, yb, sl 1, yfwd, turn.
5th row: Sl 1, k22, yfwd, sl 1, yb, turn.
6th row: Sl 1, p26, yb, sl 1, yfwd, turn.
7th row: Sl 1, k30, yfwd, sl 1, yb, turn.
8th row: Sl 1, p34, yb, sl 1, yfwd, turn.
9th row: Sl 1, k38, yfwd, sl 1, yb, turn.
10th row: Sl 1, p42, yb, sl 1, yfwd, turn.
11th row: Sl 1, k37, yfwd, sl 1, yb, turn.
12th row: Sl 1, p32, yb, sl 1, yfwd, turn.
13th row: Sl 1, k27, yfwd, sl 1, yb, turn.
14th row: Sl 1, p22, yb, sl 1, yfwd, turn.
15th row: Sl 1, k19, yfwd, sl 1, yb, turn.
16th row: Sl 1, p16, yb, sl 1, yfwd, turn.
17th row: Sl 1, k33, yfwd, sl 1, yb, turn.
18th row: Sl 1, p50, yb, sl 1, yfwd, turn.
Shape face: 1st dec row: Sl 1, k1, k2tog, [k5, k2tog] 7 times, k4, turn and cast on 4 sts. (60 sts.) Mark each end of last row. St st 3 rows.
2nd dec row: K8, k2tog, [k4, k2tog] 7 times, k8. (52 sts.) P 1 row.
3rd dec row: K4, k2tog, [k4, k2tog] 7 times, k4. (44 sts.) P 1 row.
4th dec row: [K3, k2tog] 8 times, k4. (36 sts.) P 1 row. Bind off tightly.

Shape snout With RS facing, pick up and k 36 sts along bind off row. Beg with a p row, st st 3 rows.
1st dec row: [K4, k2tog] 6 times. (30 sts.) St st 3 rows.
2nd dec row: [K2tog, k3] 6 times. (24 sts.) P 1 row.
3rd dec row: [K1, k2tog] 8 times. (16 sts.)
4th dec row: [P2tog] 8 times. (8 sts.) Break off yarn, leaving a long end. Thread end through rem sts, pull up and secure.

EARS (make 4)
With 7 (4½ mm) needles and Black, cast on 13 sts. St st 4 rows. Dec 1 st at each end of next row, then EOR twice. (7 sts.) Dec 1 st at each end of next row. (5 sts.) Bind off.

NOSE (make 1)
With 7 (4½ mm) needles and Black, cast on 5 sts. St st 3 rows. Dec 1 st at each end of next row. Work 3tog and fasten off.

EYE PATCHES
With 7 (4½ mm) needles and Black, cast on 5 sts. K 1 row. Cont in st st, inc 1 st at each end of next 2 rows. (9 sts.) St st 7 rows.
Next row: Dec, k to end.
Next row: P to last 2 sts, dec. Dec 1 st at each end of next 2 rows. (3 sts.) Bind off. Make one more, reversing shapings by reading p for k and k for p.

FINISHING
Join sides of body pieces together from top of leghole to beginning of armhole shaping. Sew in front crotch gusset to lower edge of back, matching markers.
Join leg seams, with this seam running at center of inside of each leg, join together bind-off sts of instep. Sew in soles.
Join row ends of arms, then with this seam running at center of inside of each arm, join together cast-on edge. Sew legs and arms in place. Stuff legs, body and arms firmly.
Join head seam from marker to top of snout. Stuff head firmly. With the end of head seam at center of front neck of body, stitch head in place. Join paired ear pieces together, position on head and sew in place.
Sew on nose piece, then with Black, embroider mouth. Position eye patches on head and stitch in place. Using White, embroider circle of 7 chain stitches on each patch for eyes.

Rabbits

Worked in a fluffy tweed yarn, these cuddly rabbits will delight any child. Knit practical overalls or a pretty little dress for a day's outing, then later snuggle down and go to sleep with these loveable rabbits. Sweet dreams.

SKILL LEVEL 3

MEASUREMENTS
Large rabbit is approximately 15½ in. (39 cm) tall
Small rabbit is approximately 8 in. (20 cm) tall

MATERIALS
- 3 x 50 g balls of Rowan Kid Classic in Gray
- Scraps of Rowan Kid Classic in Pale Pink and Pale Blue
- 1 x 50 g ball of Jaeger Baby Merino DK in Blue
- 1 x 50 g ball of Jaeger Baby Merino DK in Pink
- Scraps of black and pale pink embroidery thread
- Pair each of 3 (3¼ mm), 5 (3¾ mm) and 6 (4 mm) knitting needles
- 3 small buttons

ABBREVIATIONS
See page 14.

GAUGE
20 sts and 27 rows to 4 in. (10 cm) measured over stockinette stitch using 5 (3¾ mm) needles.

LARGE RABBIT
LEGS (make 2)
With 5 (3¾ mm) needles and Gray, cast on 24 sts.
P 1 row.
Next row: K1, [m1, k1] to end. (47 sts.)
P 1 row.
Next row: K1, m1, k20, [m1, k1] 6 times, k19, m1, k1. (55 sts.)
Work 7 rows.
Next row: K25, k2tog, k1, skp, k25.
P 1 row.

Next row: K24, k2tog, k1, skp, k24.
P 1 row.
Next row: K23, k2tog, k1, skp, k23.
P 1 row.
Next row: K22, k2tog, k1, skp, k22. (47 sts.)
P 1 row.
Next row: K13, bind off next 21 sts, k to end.
Work 17 rows in st st across all 26 sts.
Next row: K3, k2tog, k3, skp, k5, k2tog, k3, skp, k4.
P 1 row.
Next row: K2, k2tog, k3, skp, k3, k2tog, k3, skp, k3. (18 sts.)
P 1 row. Bind off.

BODY
Begin at neck edge.
With 5 (3¾ mm) needles and Gray, cast on 33 sts.
P 1 row.
Next row: k1, [m1, k1] to end. (65 sts.)
Beg with a p row, work 5 rows in st st.
Next row: [K8, m1] 4 times, k1, [m1, k8] 4 times. (73 sts.)
Work 3 rows.
Next row: K36, m1, k1, m1, k36. (75 sts.)
Work 35 rows.
Next row: K35, skp, k1, k2tog, k35.
Work 3 rows.
Next row: K34, skp, k1, k2tog, k34.
Work 3 rows.
Next row: K33, skp, k1, k2tog, k33.
Work 3 rows.
Next row: K32, skp, k1, k2tog, k32.
Work 3 rows.
Next row: K31, skp, k1, k2tog, k31. (65 sts.)
P 1 row.
Bind off.

ARMS (make 2)

With 5 (3¾ mm) needles and Gray, cast on 6 sts.
P 1 row.
Next row: K1, [m1, k1] to end. (11 sts.)
Rep last 2 rows once more. (21 sts.)
P 1 row.
Next row: K1, [m1, k4, m1, k1] 4 times. (29 sts.)
P 1 row.
Next row: K1, [m1, k6, m1, k1] 4 times. (37 sts.)
Work 15 rows.
Next row: K1, [skp, k13, k2tog, k1] twice. (33 sts.)
Work 3 rows.
Inc 1 st at each end of next row. (35 sts.)
Work 19 rows.
Next row: K1, [skp, k12, k2tog, k1] twice. (31 sts.)
P 1 row.
Next row: K1, [skp, k10, k2tog, k1] twice. (27 sts.)
P 1 row.
Next row: K1, [k2tog] to end. (14 sts.)

P 1 row.
Next row: [K2tog] to end. (7 sts.)
Break yarn, thread through rem sts, pull up tightly
and fasten off securely.
Sew underarm seam, leaving an opening.
Stuff firmly and close opening.

HEAD

With 5 (3¾ mm) needles and Gray, cast on 7 sts.
P 1 row.
Next row: K1, [m1, k1] to end.
Rep the last 2 rows twice more. (49 sts.)
Work 3 rows in st st.
Next row: K1, [m1, k3] to end. (65 sts.)
Work 3 rows.
Next row: K1, [m1, k4] to end. (81 sts.)
Work 5 rows.
Next row: K1, skp, k35, k2tog, k1, skp, k35, k2tog, k1.
P 1 row.
Next row: K1, skp, k33, k2tog, k1, skp, k33, k2tog, k1.
P 1 row.
Next row: K1, skp, k31, k2tog, k1, sko, k31, k2tog, k1.
(69 sts.)
P 1 row.
Next row: K1, skp, k29, k2tog, k1, skp, k29, k2tog, k1.
P 1 row.
Next row: K1, skp, k27, k2tog, k1, skp, k27, k2tog, k1.
P 1 row.
Next row: K1, skp, k25, k2tog, k1, skp, k25, k2tog, k1.
(57 sts.)
P 1 row.
Next row: K1, [skp] 6 times, k1, [k2tog] 7 times, k1,
[skp] 7 times, k1, [k2tog] 6 times, k1. (31 sts.)
P 1 row.
Next row: K1, [skp] 3 times, k2, [k2tog] 3 times, k1,
[skp] 3 times, k2, [k2tog] 3 times, k1. (19 sts.)
P 1 row.
Next row: K1, [skp] twice, [k2tog] twice, k1, [skp]
twice, [k2tog] twice, k1. (11 sts.)
P 1 row.
Next row: K1, skp, k2tog, k1, skp, k2tog, k1. (7 sts.)
P 1 row.
Break yarn, thread through rem sts, pull up tightly
and fasten off securely.

EARS (make 2)
Outer Ears

With 5 (3¾ mm) needles and Gray, cast on 20 sts.
Work 26 rows st st.
Dec 1 st at each end of next row, then EOR until 2 sts
rem.

Work 2 tog and fasten off.

Inner Ears

With 5 (3¾ mm) needles and Pale Pink, cast on 18 sts.
Work 26 rows in st st.
Dec 1 st at each end of next row, then EOR until 2 sts rem.
Work 2 tog and fasten off. Join ears into pairs.

FINISHING

Fold sides of body to center, join bind-off edge. Gather neck edge of body, pull up and secure. Sew back seam, leaving an opening. Stuff firmly and close opening. Sew head in position. Sew ears in place. Attach arms and legs. Embroider French knots for eyes and stem stitch for mouth using Black. Embroider nose in satin stitch using Pink.

SMALL RABBIT

LEGS (make 2)

With 5 (3¾ mm) needles and Gray, cast on 12 sts.
P 1 row.
Next row: K1, [m1, k1] to end. (23 sts.)
P 1 row.
Next row: K1, m1, k8, [m1, k1] 6 times, k7, m1, k1. (31 sts.)
Work 3 rows.
Next row: K13, k2tog, k1, skp, k13.
P 1 row.
Next row: K12, k2tog, k1, skp, k12. (27 sts.)
P 1 row.
Next row: K7, bind off next 13 sts, k to end.
Work 7 rows in st st across all 14 sts.
Next row: K1, k2tog, k1, skp, k2, k2tog, k1, skp, k1. (10 sts.)
P 1 row.
Bind off.

BODY

Begin at neck edge.
With 5 (3¾ mm) needles and Gray, cast on 15 sts.
P 1 row.
Next row: K1, [m1, k1] to end. (29 sts.)
Beg with a p row work 5 rows in st st.
Next row: [K7, m1] twice, k1, [m1, k7] twice. (33 sts.)
Work 3 rows.
Next row: K16, m1, k1, m1, k16.
Work 17 rows.
Next row: K15, skp, k1, k2tog, k15.
Work 3 rows.
Next row: K14, skp, k1, k2tog, k14. (31 sts.)
P 1 row.
Bind off.

ARMS (make 2)

With 5 (3¾ mm) needles and Gray, cast on 6 sts.
P 1 row.
Next row: K1, [m1, k1] to end. (11 sts.)
P 1 row.
Next row: K1, [m1, k4, m1, k1] twice. (15 sts.)
Work 7 rows.
Next row: K1, [skp, k2, k2tog, k1] twice. (11 sts.)
Work 3 rows.
Inc one st at each end of next row. (13 sts.)
Work 5 rows.
Next row: K1, [skp, k1, k2tog, k1] twice. (9 sts.)
P 1 row.
Next row: K1, [k2tog] to end. (5 sts.)
Break yarn, thread through rem sts, pull up and fasten off securely.

Join underarm seam, leaving an opening.
Stuff firmly and close opening.

HEAD

With 5 (3¾ mm) needles and Gray, cast on 7 sts.
P 1 row.
Next row: K1, [m1, k1] to end.
Rep the last 2 rows once more. (25 sts.)
Work 3 rows in st st.
Next row: K1, [m1, k3] to end. (33 sts.)
Work 3 rows.
Next row: K1, [m1, k4] to end. (41 sts.)
P 1 row.
Next row: K1, skp, k15, k2tog, k1, skp, k15, k2tog, k1.
P 1 row.
Next row: K1, skp, k13, k2tog, k1, skp, k13, k2tog, k1.
P 1 row.
Next row: K1, skp, k11, k2tog, k1, skp, k11, k2tog, k1.
(29 sts.)
P 1 row.
Next row: K1, [skp] 3 times, k1, [k2tog] 3 times, k1,
[skp] 3 times, k1, [k2tog] 3 times, k1. (17 sts.)

P 1 row.
Next row: K1, skp, sl 1, k2tog, psso, k2tog, k1, skp, sl
1, k2tog, psso, k2tog, k1. (11 sts.)
P 1 row.
Break yarn, thread through rem sts, pull up and
fasten off securely.

EARS (make 2)
Outer Ears
With 5 (3¾ mm) needles and Gray, cast on 14 sts.
Work 20 rows in st st.
Dec 1 st at each end of next row, then EOR until 2 sts
rem.
Work 2 tog and fasten off.
Inner Ears
With 5 (3¾ mm) needles and Pale Blue, cast on 12 sts.
Work 20 rows in st st.
Dec 1 st at each end of next row, then EOR until 2 sts
rem.
Work 2 tog and fasten off. Join ears together in pairs.

FINISHING
Work as for Large Rabbit, noting that purl side of
work is RS.

DRESS
FRONT
With 3 (3¼ mm) needles and Pink, cast on 42 sts.
K 3 rows.
Change to 6 (4 mm) needles.
Cont in st st.
Work 16 rows.
Dec row: K1, *k2tog; rep from * to last st, k1. (22 sts.)
Change to 3 (3¼ mm) needles.
K 3 rows.
Change to 6 (4 mm) needles. **
St st 4 rows.
Next row: K to end.
Next row: K3, p to last 3 sts, k3.
Rep the last 2 rows 3 more times .
Change to 3 (3¼ mm) needles.
K 4 rows.
Bind off.

BACK
Work as given for front to **.
Next row: K11, turn.
Next row: K2, p to end.
Next row: K11, turn.
Next row: K2, p to end.
Next row: K11, turn.

Next row: K2, p to last 3 sts, k3.
Rep the last 2 rows 3 more times .
Change to 3 (3¼ mm) needles.
K 4 rows.
Cast off.
With RS facing, rejoin yarn to rem sts.
Next row: K11.
Next row: P to last sts, k2.
Next row: K11.
Next row: P to last sts, k2.
Next row: K11.
Next row: K3, p to last 2 sts, k2.
Rep the last 2 rows 3 more times .
Change to 3 (3¼ mm) needles.
K 2 rows.
Buttonhole row: K1, yo, k2tog, k to end.
K 1 row.
Bind off.
Join shoulder seams, leaving 1½ in. (4 cm) open for
neck. Join side seams. Sew on button.

OVERALLS

With 3 (3¼ mm) needles and Blue, cast on 40 sts.
K 3 rows.
Change to 6 (4 mm) needles.
Cont in st st.
Work 12 rows.
Cast on 6 sts at beg of next 2 rows. (52 sts.)
St st 26 rows.
Change to 3 (3¼ mm) needles.
K 4 rows.
Bind off 36 sts, k to end. (16 sts.)
Change to 6 (4 mm) needles.
Next row: P to last 3 sts, k3.

Next row: K2, skp, k to end.
Rep the last 2 rows 7 more times and first row again.
(7 sts.)
Work 2 rows even.
Change to 3 (3¼ mm) needles.
K 2 rows.
Buttonhole row: K2, yo, k2tog, k to end.
K 1 row.
  Bind off.
    Work a second leg to match, reversing all shapings.

STRAPS (make 2)

With 3 (3¼ mm) needles and Blue, cast on 4 sts.
Cont in g st until strap measures 8½ in. (22 cm).
Bind off.

FINISHING

Sew center front and center back seams. Sew inside
leg seams. Attach one end of each strap to upper
edge of back 1 in. (2.5 cm) from center seam. Attach
buttons securely to other ends of straps.

Clown

This colorful clown is sure to provide lots of fun and amusement with his cheery colors, smiling face, and big red nose.

MEASUREMENTS
Approximately 16 in. (41 cm) high

MATERIALS
- 2 x 50 g balls of Rowan Handknit DK Cotton in each of Pale Pink and Yellow
- 1 x 50 g ball of Rowan Handknit DK Cotton in each of White, Red, Blue, Green and Orange
- Pair of 3 (3¼ mm), 5 (3¾ mm) and 6 (4 mm) knitting needles
- Washable toy stuffing
- Size D (3.25 mm) crochet hook

ABBREVIATIONS
See page 14.

GAUGE
22 sts and 30 rows to 4 in. (10 cm) measured over stockinette stitch using 5 (3¾ mm) needles.

DOLL
BACK
With 5 (3¾ mm) needles and Pale Pink, cast on 35 sts.
Beg with a k row, work 40 rows in st st.
Mark each end of last row with a colored thread.
** Work another 49 rows.
Next row: P16, bind off next 3 sts, p to end.
Cont in stripes of 4 rows White and 4 rows Orange.
Cont on last set of sts for first leg.
Work 40 rows in st st.
Mark each end of last row. **
Cont in White only.
Work 6 rows.
Shape Heel
Next row: K8, skp, k1, turn.
Next row: P2, p2tog, p1, turn.
Next row: K3, skp, k1, turn.

Next row: P4, p2tog, p1, turn.
Cont in this way, dec one st as established on every row until 10 sts rem, ending with a p row.
Leave these sts on a holder.
Beg with 4 rows White, now cont in stripes of 4 rows Orange and 4 rows White.
With right side facing and beg at marker, pick up and k 6 sts from side of heel, k10 sts from holder, pick up and k 6 sts from other side of heel to marker. (22 sts.)
Cont in st st, dec one st at each end of every 4th row 3 times. (16 sts.)
Work 11 rows, ending with 4 rows Orange.
Shape Toes
*** Cont in White only.
Next row: K1, skp, k to last 3 sts, k2tog, k1.
P 1 row.
Rep last 2 rows once more. (12 sts.)
K 1 row.
Next 2 rows: P9, turn, k to end.
Next 2 rows: P6, turn, k to end. ***
Leave these sts on a spare needle.
With right side facing, rejoin yarn to rem sts for second leg and work as given for first leg, reversing shaping.

FRONT
With 5 (3¾ mm) needles and Pale Pink, cast on 35 sts.
Beg with a k row, work 22 rows in st st.
Next row: K12 in Pale Pink, 11 White, 12 Pale Pink.
Next row: P10 in Pale Pink, 15 White, 10 Pale Pink.
Next row: K8 in Pale Pink, 19 White, 8 Pale Pink.
Next row: P7 in Pale Pink, 21 White, 7 Pale Pink.
Next row: K6 in Pale Pink, 23 White, 6 Pale Pink.
Next row: P6 in Pale Pink, 23 White, 6 Pale Pink.
Rep the last 2 rows five more times .
Next row: Using Pale Pink, K to end.
Next row: Using Pale Pink, P to end.
Mark each end of last row with a colored thread.
Work as given for Back from ** to **.
Work another 24 rows in st st.

P 1 row.
Next row: K13, m1, k3, m1, k13.
P 1 row.
Next row: K13, m1, k5, m1, k13. (33 sts.)
P 1 row.
Next row: K20, turn and cast on one st.
Next row: P8, turn and cast on one st.
Work 4 rows on these 9 sts.
Next row: K1, [k2tog] 4 times.
Break yarn, thread through rem sts, pull up, fasten off securely, then sew thumb seam.
With right side facing, rejoin yarn at base of thumb, pick up and k 2 sts from base of thumb, k to end. (28 sts.)
Work 9 rows.
Shape top
Next row: Skp, k10, k2tog, skp, k10, k2tog.
Next row: P to end.
Next row: Skp, k8, k2tog, skp, k8, k2tog.
Next row: P to end.
Next row: Skp, k6, k2tog, skp, k6, k2tog. (16 sts.)
Next row: P8, turn.
With right sides together, fold arm in half, taking 1 st from each needle and working them together, bind off.

NOSE

With 3 (3¼ mm) needles and Red, cast on 14 sts.
Beg with a k row, cont in st st.
Work 2 rows.
Next row: K1, * m1, k1; rep from * to end. (27 sts.)
Work 5 rows.
Next row: * K1, k2tog; rep from * to end. (18 sts.)
P 1 row.
Next row: * K2tog; rep from * to end.
Next row: P1, *p2tog; rep from * to end.
Thread yarn through rem sts, pull up and fasten off securely.
Sew seam.

HAIR

Using Yellow, make a selection of twisted cords 2½–5 in. (6–12 cm) long (see page 13).

FINISHING

Join back and front together, leaving cast-on edge free. Stuff firmly.
Thread a length of yarn around neck edge between markers, pull up tightly and fasten off securely.
Knot approximately 24 hair cords through cast-on edge of head.

Shape Toes
Work as given for Back from *** to ***.
With right sides of back and front together and taking 1 st from each needle and working them tog, bind off toe sts.
With right side facing, rejoin yarn to rem sts for second leg and complete as given for first leg, reversing toe shaping.

ARMS (make 2)

With 5 (3¾ mm) needles and Pale Pink, cast on 26 sts.
Beg with a k row work 34 rows in st st.
Shape thumb.
Next row: K13, m1, k13.
P 1 row.
Next row: K13, m1, k1, m1, k13.

Stuff head, gather cast-on edge, pull up and secure, join gathers to form a seam across top of head. Knot remaining hair cords around top of head.

Stuff nose lightly and sew in position.

Join arm seams, leaving end open, stuff firmly and close opening.

Sew to side seams of body.

Using Blue, embroider eyes in satin stitch. Using Red, embroider mouth in stem stitch.

SWEATER

BACK & FRONT ALIKE

With 5 (3¾ mm) needles and Blue, cast on 44 sts. K3 rows.

Cont in st st stripes of 2 rows Yellow, Red, Green, Blue; these 8 rows form patt, rep throughout until 38 rows have been worked.

Change to blue, k 5 rows. Bind off.

SLEEVES

With 5 (3¾ mm) needles and Blue, cast on 40 sts. K3 rows.

Cont in st st stripes as established for Back and Front.

Rep until 24 rows have been worked. Bind off.

FINISHING

Join Front and Back for 2 in. (5 cm) at each shoulder. Sew on sleeves. Sew side and sleeve seams.

PANTS (make 2 pieces)

With 5 (3¾ mm) needles and Yellow, cast on 58 sts. K 3 rows.

Work in st st patt using Yellow and Blue, following Chart on page 108, to end of row 39.

Using Yellow, k 3 rows.

Bind off.

Straps

With 5 (3¾ mm) needles and Yellow, cast on 5 sts.

Cont in g st until strap measures 7 in. (18 cm). Bind off.

FINISHING

Sew inner leg seams. Sew front and back seam. Sew straps in place.

Suppliers

United States

Annie's Attic
103 N. Pearl Street
Big Sandy, TX 75755
888-685-2233
www.anniesattic.com

Aunt Mary's Yarns
150 Avenue E.
Rochelle, IL 61068
877-250-9276
www.auntmarysyarns.com

Brown Sheep Company
100662 Country Road 16
Mitchell, NE 69357
306-635-2190
www.brownsheep.com

Coats & Clark
P.O. Box 12229
Greenville, SC 29612-0229
800-648-1479
www.coatsandclark.com

Cotton Clouds
800-322-7888
www.cottonclouds.com

D & R Fabric and Yarn Center
36-04 Ditmars Boulevard
Astoria, NY 11105
718-777-0182

Garden City Stitches
725 Franklin Avenue
Garden City, NY 11530
516-739-3757
GCSshop@aol.com

Knit Witts
56 Allen Road
Brookfield, MA 01506
877--8775648
www.knitwitts.com

Lion Brand Yarn
34 West 15th Street
New York, NY 10011
800-258-9276
www.lionbrand.com

Lone Star Yarns
2205 Windsor Place
Pine Bluff, AR 71603
870-536-2116
www.lonestaryarns.com

Maggie's Rags
507 Rose Avenue
Blacksburg, VA 24060
888-809-7004
www.maggiesrags.com

Marr Haven
772 39th Street
Allegan, MI 49010-9353
269-673-8800
www.marrhaven.com

Martha's Yarn Emporium
640 Isadore Street
Steven's Point, WI 54481
715-342-1911
www.marthasyarnemporium.com

Plymouth Yarn Company
P.O. Box 28
Bristol, PA 19007
215-788-0459
www.plymouthyarn.com

Schaefer Yarns
Kelly's Corners
Interlaken, NY 14847
www.schaeferyarn.com

Simtex Yarns, Inc.
214 Canal Street
Fort Plain, NY 13339
518-882-5200
www.simtex.com

Spin A Yarn
9 Mitchell Avenue
Binghamton, NY 13903
607-722-3318
www.spinayarn2knit.com

The Woolery
R.D. #1
Genoa, NY 13071
800-441-9665
www.woolery.com

Yarn Farm
11610 Township Road 180
Findlay, OH 45840
419-423-4282
www.yarnfarm.homestead.com

Yarnware.com
69 Lapis Circle
West Orange, NJ 07052
877-369-9276
www.yarnware.com

Canada

Beehive Wool Shop
1700 Douglas Street
Victoria, BC V8W 2G7
888-334-9005
www.beehivewool.com

Cabin Fever Wool & Knitting
Supplies
110 Mary Street
Orillia, ON
800-671-9112
www.cabinfever.on.ca

Elann.com
P.O. Box 18125
1269-56th Street
Delta, BC V4L 2M4
800-720-0616
www.elann.com

Four Seasons Knitting Products
89 Sarah Ashbridge Avenue
Toronto, ON M4L 3Y1
416-693-6848
www.fourseasonknitting.com

Ram Wools
1266 Fife Street
Winnipeg, MB R2X 2N6
800-263-8002
www.ramswools.com

The Wool Mill
2170 Danforth Avenue
Toronto, ON M4C 1K3
416-696-2670
walksoft@interlog.com

Acknowledgments

My special thanks go to all my family, especially Lucy and Molly.

My thanks also to the following:
everyone at Rowan Yarns; all the brilliant knitters: Tina Church, Rae Fraser, Linda Wood and Margaret Sperring; Tina Egleton; Penny Hill and Tina Church for making my toys come alive; Sue Whiting for her expert pattern checking; Shona Wood for her beautiful photography; Lisa Tai, the book designer. Finally I would like to thank Clare Sayer and Rosemary Wilkinson for all their hard work and support and for making this book possible.

Index